A Practical Guide to the Administration of Estates & Trusts

Foreword

For many years, Bank of Ireland Trust Services has acted as a professional executor and trustee in the administration of estates and trusts. It has built up a huge expertise in these areas and in this extremely useful guide, the bank gives enormous guidance and information to persons acting as executors and trustees.

Because of the increasing value of property and the Celtic Tiger, many estates and trusts now have substantial assets to administer and the obligations of executors and trustees in complying with all their legal and taxation duties can be very onerous. This guide sets out all the duties of executors and trustees in a clear and concise fashion and provides a huge amount of information which has not been made readily accessible to the public before.

In particular, the section on Trusts provides much practical guidance on areas such as trust records, trustee meetings and on the information Trust beneficiaries are legally entitled to, which can cause problems in practice.

As a solicitor practising in this area of law, I believe this guide is essential reading for anyone acting as an executor or trustee and will be of enormous benefit to professional persons such as solicitors, accountants, bankers and investment advisors who have to advise executors or trustees. The Bank of Ireland will help thousands of people and their families by publishing this guide and I commend the bank for this excellent publication.

John Costello

Chairman of the Law Society Committee on Probate and Taxation

> It should be noted that where the male gender is used, it is taken to refer to males and females.
>
> Consequently, we hope that Readers will find a universal 'he' more readable and acceptable than a 'he/she' in almost every sentence.

This book was typeset and designed by CMB Design Group

Published by
Bank of Ireland Trust Services,
Head Office,
Lower Baggot Street,
Dublin 2,
Ireland.

e-mail: boitrust@boinet.ie
Website: www.boitrust.ie

©Bank of Ireland Trust Services

ISBN: 0-9538789-0-2

All rights reserved. No reproduction, copy or transmission of this publication can be made without written permission.

While strenuous efforts have been made to ensure the accuracy of information in this book neither the publisher nor the authors are liable for any errors or omissions. Professional advice should always be sought before acting on any issue covered in this book.

Printed in the Republic of Ireland by Colorprint.

About the Authors

Rachel Curran is a law graduate of University College, Dublin and completed a masters in Commercial Law in 1994. She qualified as a solicitor in 1986 and is a founder member of the Society of Trust and Estate Practitioners in Ireland. Rachel has extensive experience in the area of administration of Trusts and Estates.
She joined Bank of Ireland in 1995.

Deirdre Dunne is Estate Planning Executive at Bank of Ireland Trust Services. Deirdre deals on a daily basis with clients on all aspects of estate planning including Trusts, Wills and Capital Taxes. Deirdre is a business studies graduate of Trinity College Dublin, an associate of the Institute of Taxation of Ireland and a committee member of the Society of Trust and Estate Practitioners in Ireland.

SECTION ONE

A PRACTICAL GUIDE TO THE ADMINISTRATION OF ESTATES — 1
Aim of this Section — 2
Role of Executor — 2
Renouncing your Appointment as Executor — 3
Reserving your Right to Act as Executor — 3
The Steps of Administration — 4

IMMEDIATE STEPS TO BE TAKEN BY THE EXECUTOR POST DEATH — 5
Ensure the Funeral is Arranged — 6
Secure the Property of the Deceased — 6
Meeting with the Beneficiaries — 8
Appoint a Solicitor/Professional Adviser — 9

THE WILL — 11
Requirements for a Valid Will — 12
Reading the Will — 13
Problems you may encounter with the Will — 14
Typical Problems associated with specific Gifts in Wills — 18
Legal Remedies to Delay or Query the Administration
  of a Particular Estate — 22
Disclaimer — 24
Wills dealing with Foreign Property — 26

INTESTACY: WHERE THERE IS NO WILL — 27
Administration of an Intestate Estate — 28
Who is entitled to benefit under Intestacy? — 29
Who can extract a Grant of Administration Intestate? — 30

IDENTIFICATION and VALUATION OF ASSETS & LIABILITIES — 33

Marketable Securities — 34
Private Company Shares — 35
Real Property — 35
Chattels/Jewellery — 35
Accounts in Banks, Building Societies and other Financial Institutions — 36
Savings Certificates/Savings Bond — 36
Prize Bonds — 36
Life Assurance Policies — 36
Company/Employee Entitlements — 37
Car — 37
Joint Bank Accounts — 37
Assets In Joint Names — 38
Assets passing outside the Will — 38
Debts — 39
Tax — 40
Social Welfare Benefits — 40

INLAND REVENUE AFFIDAVIT/ SCHEDULE OF ASSETS — 41

Probate Tax — 43
Corrective Affidavit — 43

APPLYING FOR THE GRANT OF PROBATE — 45

ACTION FOLLOWING ISSUE OF GRANT — 49

Collecting in the Assets — 50
Cash Balances — 50
Marketable Securities — 51
Private Company Shares — 51

Chattels/Jewellery	51
Savings Certificates/Savings Bonds	51
Prize Bonds	52

PAYMENT OF DEBTS   53

Taxes up to Date of Death	54
Income Tax Post Death	54
Capital Gains Tax Post Death	55
Other Debts & Liabilities	55
Statutory Notice to Creditors	55

OTHER SPECIAL ENTITLEMENTS   57

Right of Surviving Spouse under the Succession Act	58
Right of Children under the Succession Act	59
Right of Separated Spouse or Former Spouse	59

DISTRIBUTING THE ESTATE   61

"Executor's Year"	62
Solicitors and other Professional Costs	63
Receipts	64
Finalising Inheritance Tax Position	64
Specific Bequests	64
Marketable Securities	65
Private Company Shares	65
Houses and Lands	66
Charitable Donations and Bequests	66
Payment of Cash Legacies	66
In Specie and Interim Distributions to Residuary Legatees	67
In Specie Distributions of Shares	67
Interim and Final Distributions to Residuary Legatees	69

FINAL ACCOUNTS   71

Residuary Trust Funds	73

SECTION TWO

A PRACTICAL GUIDE TO THE ADMINISTRATION OF TRUSTS	75
THE ROLE OF THE TRUSTEE	76
WHAT IS A TRUST?	77
DUTIES OF TRUSTEES	81
POWERS OF TRUSTEES	85
Power of Sale	86
Power to Give Receipts	86
Power to Insure Buildings	87
Power to Renew Leases	87
Power to Compound Liabilities	87
Power to Delegate	87
Power of Advancement	88
TRUST ADMINISTRATION	89
Reading a Trust Deed	90
Requirements for a Valid Trust	91
Collecting in the Trust Property	92
Trust Records	94
Correspondence File	94
Permanent Documents File	96
Financial File	97
TAXATION	99
Income Tax	100
Capital Gains Tax	101
Capital Acquisitions Tax	102
Discretionary Trust Taxes	104
Tax on Charitable Trusts	105
Table of Tax and Payment Deadlines	106

TRUST ACCOUNTS — 107
- Financial Statements — 109
- Providing Information to Beneficiaries — 112
- Trustees Remuneration — 114
- Trustees Expenses — 115

TRUSTEES MEETINGS — 117

INVESTMENT OF TRUST ASSETS — 119
- Does the Trust Deed give you power to invest in all types of Investments? — 120
- Do you have power to employ Investment Advisers? — 121
- Setting Investment Objectives — 121
- Choosing an Investment Adviser — 122
- Investment Management Agreement — 124
- Monitoring Investment Performance — 125
- Transactions in Trust Assets — 126
- Freehold & Leasehold Property — 127
- Private Company Shares — 130
- Chattels and Works of Art — 132
- Loans — 133

APPOINTMENT, REMOVAL AND RETIREMENT OF TRUSTEES — 135
- Appointment — 136
- Removal of Trustees — 137
- Retirement of Trustees — 138

GLOSSARY — 139

SECTION ONE

A Practical Guide to the Administration of Estates

Aim of this Section

Our aim in this section is to guide inexperienced executors through the various steps of Administration of Estates in a practical and clear manner. While you will need to enlist the help of professionals - solicitors, tax advisers etc., we hope this book will provide you with enough knowledge to enable you to participate actively in the Administration, rather than having solely to rely on advice from others. We have tried to write the text in plain and easy to understand English, although it is impossible to avoid the use of legal terms at certain times. To help you in this regard, we have included a glossary of common legal terms for easy reference at the back of this book.

Role of Executor

Before deciding whether to accept your appointment as Executor, you should be familiar with what the role entails. In simple terms, the Executor is the person who ensures that the directions as recorded by the Testator in his Will, are carried through. Before you accept the appointment of Executor, you should be happy that you have the time and energy to see the job through. Most administrations take up to a year to complete although this depends on the complexity of the Will and the type of Assets in the Estate. As Executor, you should always act impartially and independently, if you feel that due to a vested interest in the Estate it may be difficult for you to do so you may consider allowing a non-interested party to take over the role. For example, if the testator held shares in a private company of which you are a director, it may not be possible for you to act independently. Just because you have been appointed under the Will as Executor does not mean that you have to accept the appointment. It is open to you to renounce or reserve your rights to act.

Renouncing your Appointment as Executor

If you renounce, then all rights to participate in the administration of the deceased's Estate are lost to you. It is vital that before dealing with any of the Assets of the Estate, you make up your mind whether you are going to accept the appointment of Executor. Should you interfere with the assets of an Estate, you may be accused of intermeddling with the Estate and may lose your right to renounce the appointment. You may only be able to extricate yourself at this stage by going to court.

Reserving your Right to Act as Executor

If you are one of two or more Executors, then it is possible to simply reserve your right to act, this will allow you the opportunity to come back at a later stage to participate in the administration if, for example, you are not satisfied with the progress being made etc.

The Steps of Administration:

In summary, the following tasks must be undertaken to administer an Estate:

1. Examine the Will.
2. Meet with the beneficiaries.
3. Identify and value the Assets and Liabilities of the Deceased.
4. Protect the Assets of the Estate through the course of administration.
5. Prepare Inland Revenue Affidavit and submit to Revenue Commissioners.
6. Lodge papers for Grant of Probate.
7. Grant issues.
8. Collect Assets.
9. Discharge Liabilities.
10. Identify and discharge Tax Liabilities.
11. Distribute Assets.
12. Discharge Administration Costs.
13. Prepare Accounts.

Immediate Steps to be taken by the Executor Post Death

Having decided to accept your appointment as Executor, your first task is to get a copy of the last Will. You should immediately check whether or not the deceased left any specific burial instructions. As Executor, it is your responsibility to carry out the following:

Ensure the Funeral is Arranged
(as per the deceased's instructions, if any).
An undertaker should be consulted, he will usually take care of the death notices and the grave plot etc. Money for the funeral expenses should be released from a Bank Account in the Testator's name on production of receipts by you to the Bank. All other monies held in the deceased's name will be frozen until issue of the Grant of Probate.

Secure the Property of the Deceased
Take immediate steps to secure the assets of the Testator by visiting the residence and any other property which they own. You should make sure that all are adequately insured and take an inventory of any valuable contents. The insurance company should be notified of the death of the insured person. Items for specific bequests should be identified, labelled and valued prior to distribution.

Personal papers which would include all personal correspondence, financial details including bank statements and share certificates etc. may be removed for further investigation.

In the event that the contents are in an unoccupied house, any valuable contents should be put in storage as soon as possible. In relation to a vacant property it is advisable to have the property checked over once a week by a friend, neighbour or the Gardaí.

If there are household employees of the Testator still carrying out their duties, their contracts should be investigated and if necessary short term arrangements should be made to allow the administration to proceed. If there are tenants, legal advice should be sought.

The financial situation of dependants should be ascertained and monies made available for their day to day living expenses where appropriate. You should open an Executors Bank account to deal with all immediate expenses.

Communication should be established with the beneficiaries under the Will to advise them that they are to benefit and to obtain their personal details for future correspondence.

Meeting with the Beneficiaries

Shortly after the funeral, it is helpful to meet with the beneficiaries. You should cover the following topics at the meeting.

- Your role as Executor and the steps of administration.
- The contents of the Will can be briefed to the beneficiaries.
  (The only people entitled to copies of the Will are beneficiaries entitled to a share of the residue of the estate and your co-executors, if any.)
- The financial situation of the dependants and the arrangements that need to be made for them.
- The right of the Testator's family to contest the Will. Should this arise, provision may have to be made for them which in turn could affect the terms of the Will. This is explained in more detail on pages 58 to 60 .

Obtain as much information as you can about the Testator's affairs including

- Marital status.
- List of professional Advisers to him.
- Position regarding his employees, if any.
- RSI numbers and details of prior benefits of all beneficiaries for the purpose of completing Inheritance Tax Returns.

Appoint a Solicitor/Professional Adviser

For the purposes of extracting the Grant of Probate, you should engage the services of a solicitor. Alternatively you may decide to make a personal application to the Probate office. However unless the estate is straightforward it is advisable to instruct a solicitor. At the initial consultation, the Solicitor should clearly explain the fee structure for legal services necessary for his involvement in the administration of the Estate. The fee structure you negotiate with the Solicitor should be confirmed in writing to you after the initial consultation.

The Will

Requirements for a Valid Will

As Executor you should check the Will to ensure it is the last Will written by the Testator before he died and that it is legally valid. If you are in any doubt as to the legal validity of the Will, you should discuss this with your Solicitor. Obviously the Will does not take effect until the death of the testator. Where a Will has been revoked during the lifetime of the testator by a later Will, or by a subsequent marriage the Will is no longer valid. A Will need not be in any special form, but to be legally valid it must have the following attributes:

1. The Will must be in writing.
2. The testator must be over 18 years unless married.
3. He must be of sound disposing mind.
4. He must sign his name, make his mark or acknowledge his signature in the presence of two witnesses present together. An Executor is admissible as a witness.
5. His signature or mark must be at the end of the Will.
6. The two witnesses must sign their names in his presence and in the presence of each other.
7. If the beneficiary or his or her spouse witnesses a Will the benefit to such witness is void but the Will remains valid.

Reading The Will

Your role as Executor in administering an Estate is to give effect to the testator's intention according to the written terms of the Will. The Will itself is the primary evidence of the testator's intention. The following are some rules of interpretation which are used when reading a Will.

If the Wording of the Will is Confusing
If the words used by the Testator are clear and unambiguous that is generally the end of the matter and effect must be given to the words used. If however reading the Will as a whole reveals that particular words do not accurately reflect the testator's intention, it may be necessary to go to Court to give effect to the Testator's intention.

Meaning of Words and Phrases
The general rule is that a testator is presumed to have intended that a word or a phrase is to be given its ordinary grammatical meaning unless there is something in the context or other admissible circumstances which prove otherwise.

Technical Words
When a Testator uses technical terms in his Will he is presumed to have intended them to be given their usual technical meaning, which is a question of fact to be determined from expert evidence.

The Will

A testator who does not have the benefit of professional legal advice when drawing up his Will, may use words which have a popular connotation. The words may not coincide with a technical legal connotation and if his intention is not apparent on the face of the Will, or ascertainable from the circumstances surrounding the making of the Will, the technical meaning will prevail.

Extrinsic Evidence

If there is uncertainty or ambiguity around the terms of a Will, it is possible to apply to the High Court for assistance in interpreting the Will. The so called "armchair principle" allows the Court to take cognisance of the facts and circumstances by which the testator was surrounded when he made his Will to assist in arriving at his intention.

Problems You May Encounter With The Will

Take care to ensure that the original Will is maintained in exactly the same condition in which you first receive it.

Where a Will is Damaged or Torn

If the Will has a torn edge, any staple mark, pin hole, clip mark or traces of sticky tape or glue, evidence will be required by the Probate Office stating how such damage occurred and also stating that nothing was attached to the Will or Codicil.

There are a number of people who may give this evidence i.e. an attesting witness, the person responsible for the mark or the tear, the person in whose custody the Will was retained or the person who found the Will.

Alterations in a Will

Any alterations to a Will must be authenticated at the time of making the Will in one of the following ways:

- By the signatures or initials of the testator and witnesses in the margin
- By the signatures of the testator and witnesses to a memo referring to the alteration
- By the initials of the witnesses, if the alterations are not material
- By a Codicil which refers to the alteration
- If the alterations to a Will are not authenticated as set out above, evidence on Affidavit will be required by the Probate Office when proving the Will

Lost Wills

When a Testator is known to have made a Will which cannot be found, there is a presumption that the testator destroyed it. This presumption can be set aside by contrary evidence.

The person seeking to prove the lost Will (i.e. have it admitted to probate) must establish:-

firstly that the Will was duly executed and
secondly the contents of the Will

The evidence of execution may be given by an attesting witness or someone who was present at the time the Will was executed. Evidence of the contents of the Will may be proved in a number of ways, *for example:*

> The original Will may have been drawn up by a Solicitor and an Attendance Record kept or an Instruction Sheet taken.
>
> Alternatively a person who may have read the Will and is aware of the contents may give evidence.

Where the original Will cannot be found, it is necessary for an application to be made to the Court which, if satisfied, will make an Order to prove the Will in terms of a copy. The Grant will be limited until the original or a more authentic copy thereof is lodged in the Probate Office.

If there is a photocopy available, a photocopy Will may be admitted to proof provided you are in a position to give evidence as to the continued existence, unrevoked, of the original at the date of death of the Testator. This can be a difficult problem in practice and you have to be extremely careful with your dealings in relation to beneficiaries.

No Attestation Clause at the Bottom of the Will
The absence of an Attestation Clause does not render a Will invalid but it does raise questions as to the validity of the execution. The witnesses should be ascertained and their current addresses sought. If the witnesses are not alive, enquiries should be made as there may be another witness who did not actually sign their name to the Will, but, who may have been present at the time the Will was made and who can give evidence as to the execution of the Will.

A Weak Signature
Where the signature of the testator is weak or feeble or there is some doubt as to its authenticity, the Probate Officer may require evidence that the testator was of sound disposing mind but, due to some physical infirmity, was not able to make a strong signature. Where, however, the testator dies in hospital, or where the Will was made while the testator was seriously ill, or where any doubt arises about a testator's mental capacity, the Probate Officer may require evidence as to his Testamentary Capacity.

One person who can give such evidence is the doctor who was attending the testator at the time he made the Will. If this medical evidence is not forthcoming, then the person who wrote the Will or any other responsible person who can give conclusive evidence about the testator's mental capacity at that time, may give that evidence.

Typical Problems Associated with Specific Gifts in Wills

Identification of Beneficiary

Sometimes it is not always clear as to who the Testator intended to benefit. It is a reasonable assumption that a person who conforms to the description in the Will at the date it is signed is the intended beneficiary. This presumption will give way to a contrary intention expressed by the testator in the Will. Consequently in the case of a gift to "my wife", there is a strong presumption that the intended donee is the person who is married to the testator at the date of the Will.

Gifts to a Class of People

Where the Will includes a benefit to a class of people, only those ascertained to be part of the class at the date of the death of the testator can take under the terms of the Will. For example: I give a legacy of £10,000 to each of my grandchildren living at the date of my death.

Conditions Attached to Gifts

It is not uncommon for a testator to impose a condition on a gift in his Will. If the conditions of the gift do not affect the constitutional rights of others and are otherwise consistent with fair principles they should be enforced.

Gift of Personal Effects

Quite often Testators make a specific bequest of their personal effects. The meaning of personal effects will depend on the context of the Will. It is generally taken to mean physical chattels having some personal connection with the Testator such as articles of personal or domestic use, clothing, furniture etc. but not money or securities for money. It is worth noting that collections of books, antiques, maps, clocks, watches, stamps and coins kept by Testator as hobbies have all been held to be within the definition of personal chattels, notwithstanding that the value might be such that they might be regarded as investments.

Predeceased Beneficiaries

Where a beneficiary of a specific gift named in the Will dies in the lifetime of the testator the gift lapses into residue and is distributed according to the terms of the residuary clause or if none, on intestacy. Where a residuary beneficiary dies in the lifetime of the testator, the benefit will be distributed under intestacy rules unless otherwise provided for in the Will.

There is one exception: if the benefit is to a child or grandchild of the testator, and he dies in the lifetime of the testator, leaving issue, the benefit does not lapse but is distributed according to the terms of the deceased child's Will/Intestacy.

Gifts Not Capable of Being Implemented

Where a Testator disposes of property during his lifetime which is the subject of a specific bequest or devise under the Will, the bequest or devise is no longer capable of being implemented and you cannot, for example, compensate by applying other assets or money.

Beneficiaries with Pre-Death Benefits from the Testator
(Advancement)

Before informing a Residuary beneficiary of a potential share in an Estate, it is important that you check if the Testator gave monies or other gifts to any of his children during his lifetime.

If such gifts have been made, this is known as advancement.

Advancement for the purposes of the Succession Act means a gift intended to make permanent provision for the beneficiary. It would not include maintenance payments or normal payments out of Income.

Where you establish that a child has received an advancement, that advancement is to be treated as having been made towards satisfaction of the child's share under the Will. The value of the advancement is to be ascertained at the date of the gift and not at the date of death of the testator.

The effect of the advancement rule is to determine whether the child can take any additional sum from the deceased's estate. If the advancement paid to the child is equal to or greater than the share due to the child under the Will, the child will be precluded from taking any benefit from the estate but will not have to repay the advancement in part or in full. If the advancement is less than the share due to the child from the estate then the child is entitled to the difference between the two to bring his share up to the requisite level. The onus of proving that an advancement has been made is upon the person so asserting unless the advancement has been expressed in writing by the deceased.

Legal Remedies to Delay or Query the Administration of a Particular Estate

Caveat

Any person who wishes to oppose the issue of the Grant of Probate may lodge a caveat in the probate office or any district probate registry.

A Caveat is a written notice to the Court entered through the Probate Office instructing that nothing is done with the Estate of a deceased person without prior notice to the party entering the Caveat or to his solicitor. The effect of a Caveat is to prevent the issue of the Grant of Probate.

Once the caveat has been lodged and the Grant of Probate is applied for, a Warning will issue directing the person who entered the caveat to enter a reply to the warning (called an appearance). In default of his so doing the Caveat will cease to have any effect. A Caveat remains in force for six months after which it expires and is then of no effect. However Caveats may be renewed from time to time.

The Will

A Caveat is disposed of or lost:-

(a) by lapse of time (six months) if not warned

(b) by voluntary withdrawal by the caveator

(c) by Order of Court setting it aside particularly in intestacy cases

(d) by proving a Will

(e) by no appearance to a Warning

(f) by order of the Probate Officer on consent of all parties and their solicitors (after a Warning has been entered)

Citations

Where an executor has failed in his duty to extract the grant of probate, one remedy open to a person who has an interest in the Estate is to organise for a citation to issue. A citation is a document issued by the Court calling on another person, such as the Executor or any other person entitled in priority to a Grant, to act.

Disclaimer

A beneficiary who is entitled to any benefit under a Will or upon intestacy cannot be legally forced to take the benefit and may instead disclaim it. There are various reasons why a beneficiary would choose to disclaim a benefit: out of a self interest, to benefit another beneficiary who has not been well treated under the Will or simply because the person did not like the Testator and does not wish to take anything from him under his Will.

The benefit may be disclaimed by a deed of disclaimer, by writing or may be implied from conduct. As Executor, it is advisable that you would obtain a formal renunciation by deed.

The beneficiary who disclaims an inheritance has no say as to who shall inherit after him. Once a beneficiary disclaims an inheritance it falls into the residue of the estate provided that there is a residuary clause in the Will. In the absence of such a clause the disclaimed inheritance will be distributed on intestacy. If the residuary estate is disclaimed then the residuary estate goes on intestacy.

A beneficiary may be paid a sum of money or other consideration in return for disclaiming a benefit.

A beneficiary of a single bequest cannot partially disclaim i.e. it is not possible to pick and choose among assets contained in a single bequest, it must be disclaimed as a whole or not at all. However where a beneficiary is given two separate legacies under a Will it is possible to disclaim one and take the other as long as the two are separate bequests. A residuary beneficiary cannot partially disclaim his share of the residue: it must be disclaimed as a whole or not at all.

A beneficiary may not disclaim a bequest once he has begun to receive some benefit from it. Neither will he be allowed to withdraw a disclaimer once another person has begun to receive benefit or advantage from the legacy after the disclaimer has been made. Withdrawal of a disclaimer will not be allowed where consideration was paid to the person making the disclaimer.

Tax Implications of a Disclaimer
The person who benefits as a result of the disclaimer takes the benefit from the Deceased and not the person making the disclaimer. Any consideration received by person making the disclaimer is to deemed to come from the Deceased rather than the person who actually paid the consideration.

Wills Dealing with Foreign Property

Problems can arise in relation to the validity of Wills which dispose of property located in foreign jurisdictions and foreign Wills which dispose of property located in the domestic jurisdiction. The Succession Act 1965 contains rules governing the formal validity of Wills where a foreign element is involved.

Even though the Will may not be validly executed in accordance with Irish law, it still may be valid as regards form if it complies with the internal law -

(a) of the place where it was made, or
(b) of the nationality, or
(c) the domicile of the Testator at the date the Will was made, or the date of death of the Testator, or
(d) the place where the Testator had his habitual residence, or
(e) in the case of immovable property, of the place where same is situated

The Probate Office will require evidence that the Will fulfils one of the above conditions. Such evidence must be in the form of either a sealed and certified copy of the Grant from the appropriate Court in the country concerned or an Affidavit of Law.

The Will

Intestacy:
Where there is no Will

Intestacy

Where a person dies without having made a valid Will he is said to have died intestate and his Estate is distributed according to the Succession Act.

Even where a person has made a Will, his Estate may be partly intestate in that the Will does not include instructions for the distribution of the entire Estate but only part of it. An example of this is where a person leaves cash legacies and specific bequests but does not include a clause to include the residue. Also where a Residuary beneficiary has predeceased the Testator, in some cases that benefit must be distributed according to the rules of intestacy.

Administration of an Intestate Estate

Instead of taking out a Grant of Probate and distributing the assets according to the terms of the Will, under Intestacy an Administrator must take out a Grant of Letters of Administration Intestate and follow a similar administration process as that of the Executor.

Who is Entitled to Benefit under Intestacy?

The order of entitlement to take a share in the Estate of the Intestate is set out below.

RELATIVE SURVIVING	DISTRIBUTION OF ESTATE
Spouse and children	Two-thirds to spouse, one-third equally amoung children, with children of predeceased child taking *per stirpes*
Spouse and no children.	Spouse takes all.
Children and no spouse.	Children take equally, with children of predeceased child taking *per stirpes*.
Father, mother, brothers and sisters.	Each parent takes one half.
Father, brothers and sisters.	Father takes all.
Mother, brothers and sisters.	Mother takes all.
Brothers and sisters.	All take equally. Children of predeceased brother or sister take *per stirpes*.
Nephews and nieces and grandparents.	Nephews and nieces take all equally.
Nephews and nieces uncles and aunts and great grandparents.	Nephews and nieces take all equally.
Uncles and aunts and grandparents.	Uncles and aunts take all equally.
First cousin, great uncle, great nephew and great great grandparent.	First cousin, great uncle and great nephew take all equally.

Where there is No Will: Intestacy

Who can Extract a Grant of Administration Intestate?

Any person who has a right to take a share in the Estate is entitled to extract the Grant of Administration Intestate. The order of entitlement to extract a Grant of Administration Intestate is set out below.

1. Spouse
2. Children
3. Grandchildren
4. Great Grandchildren
5. Great Great Grandchildren
6. Father - Mother
7. Brother - Sister
8. Nephew - Niece
9. Grandparents
10. Uncle - Aunt
11. Great Grandparents
12. Great Uncle / Great Aunt - First Cousin - Great Nephew / Niece
13. Great Great Grandparents

Where there is No Will: Intestacy

If the spouse, next of kin and others persons entitled to a distribution are either dead or have renounced, administration will be granted to the Personal Representative of any one of them.

Where the Personal Representatives are co-Executors, the practice is to allow any one of them to apply for a Grant reserving the rights of the other. Where they are co-Administrators, they must apply jointly, or those who do not wish to act must renounce. Administration may be granted to the child of a person who is entitled to all the Estate on renunciation and consent of such person, on that basis that such child has a hope of succeeding to his parent's Estate. Exceptionally, administration may be granted to the child of one of a number of persons entitled where they all renounce and consent.

For the remainder of this book we will refer to Executors and Wills, but the administration process is essentially the same for Intestacy.

Identification and Valuation of Assets and Liabilities

The first step in the actual administration of the Estate is to identify all assets held by the Testator. Arrangements should be made as soon as possible to obtain valuations, as at the date of death, of the assets of the deceased's Estate. These valuations will be used for the purpose of completing an Inland Revenue Affidavit which must be submitted to the Revenue. It is always wise to obtain a copy of the deceased's last Income Tax and Capital Gains Tax Returns in order to establish all securities and other Income producing assets.

The following is an outline of some of the ways the various assets may be valued:-

Marketable Securities i.e. Stocks and Shares

In general the Probate Valuation of any marketable securities is prepared by a broker on the basis of the Stock Exchange Lists as at the date of death.

It is advisable, before preparing these valuations, that formal confirmation of the holding is obtained from the Registrars of the various Companies, as lists obtained from other sources are not always accurate. If certificates are missing a letter should be written to the company Registrar for duplicates. The appropriate forms and indemnities can then be completed.

Private Company Shares (Companies not listed on the Stock Exchange)

The value of shares in Private Companies may be sought from the Secretary or Accountant of the private company concerned. If the share holding is substantial, an independent professional financial adviser should be engaged to advise on valuation methods and taxation implications. The Revenue are likely to call for copies of the most recent accounts. Therefore, it is advisable to obtain balance sheets and profit and loss accounts for three years prior to the date of death.

Real Property

It is advisable that valuations of land and house property should be obtained from appropriate auctioneers/valuers. The choice of auctioneer should be carefully considered, bearing in mind that if the property is to be sold they are likely to be the firm entrusted with handling the sale.

Chattels/Jewellery

Any personal property of the deceased which is considered to be of a substantial value should be valued by appropriate experienced valuers.

Accounts in Banks, Building Societies and other Financial Institutions

Certificates of the balances of accounts at the date of death with various institutions should be requested and, where relevant, the certificates should include details of interest accrued up to the date of death.

Savings Certificates/Savings Bonds

A letter should be written to An Post referring to the relevant item and asking for a certificate of value in respect of same.

Prize Bonds

A letter should be written to the Prize Bond office requesting a certificate of value for any Prize Bonds held by the deceased. Prize bonds are transferable and the possibility of transferring them into the name of the beneficiaries in part settlement of their share of the Estate could be considered.

Life Assurance Policies

You should ascertain if the Testator had any life policies and if so, for whose benefit they were taken out. If no beneficiary is named then the proceeds of the policy form part of the residue. The Life Assurance Company should be contacted to obtain full details of the Policies.

Enquiries should also be made to establish if there are any Section 60 Policies to cover Inheritance Tax liabilities. If so the terms should be examined to ascertain what taxes and beneficiaries are covered by the policy and also if separate Trustees of the policy were appointed by the testator. The life company will also assist you here.

Company/Employee Entitlements

Enquires should be made to the Testator's employer as to whether there are any benefits payable to the Estate, for example, death in service benefits.

Car

In the event that the Testator owned a car, it should be valued by a professional car dealer. Any subsequent sale of the car should be done in consultation with the family. Insurance arrangements should be clarified.

Joint Bank Accounts

The legal position with joint accounts is complex and it is advisable to obtain legal confirmation as to the beneficial ownership of the account before releasing any balance to the survivor.

Identification and Valuation of Assets & Liabilities

Assets in Joint Names

The legal position in relation to assets in joint names is also complex, in particular where there is real property held in the joint names of the deceased and another party. The Title Documents to same should be obtained and it should be confirmed that the property will pass correctly to the survivor of the joint owners. If in any doubt, you should obtain professional advice on the legal and taxation implications of joint ownership.

There are two main ways in which property can be held:-

Joint Tenants: If the property is owned by two or more people, on the death of one of the joint tenants it passes to the survivor(s)

Tenants in common: this is where the property is owned by two or more people, on the death of one of the owners the respective share will pass as directed under the Will of the deceased or on intestacy.

Assets Passing outside the Will

The following assets pass outside the Will but details of these will have to be included for the purpose of completing the Inland Revenue Affidavit:

- Any asset of which the Testator held a life interest only.
- Assets held in the joint names of the Testator and another individual, where it is clear that the Testator intended the other person to benefit on death.
- Death benefits passing under a life insurance policy or pension scheme where the beneficiaries are specifically named in the policy.
- Assets passing by nomination, the Testator may have left specific instructions that policy proceeds etc. be paid to a specified nominee on the death of the Testator.

Debts

You should quantify all debts of the Testator as soon as possible. It may be advisable to discharge certain debts immediately without waiting to get issue of the Grant of Probate and collection of cash balances. Many undertakers are now giving discount for early payment and this facility may be taken advantage of. In cases where individuals submit claims for expenses (e.g. cost of travel to the funeral) then legal advice may be needed as to whether or not the debts are correctly debts of the Estate.

Tax

The Testator's tax advisers, if any, should be asked for an estimate of all outstanding Income Tax and Capital Gains Tax liabilities to date of death. This should include any repayment claims for medical expenses. If the deceased was an insured person under the Social Welfare Act it should be ascertained if any Death Grant can be claimed and if so, the appropriate steps taken to claim it. The appropriate forms are available from the Post Office.

Social Welfare Benefits

Where the Testator was in receipt of benefit/assistance at any stage during his lifetime, you as Executor are personally liable for any overpayment to the deceased in the event that you distribute the proceeds of the Estate without obtaining clearance from the Department of Social Community & Family Affairs. It is therefore vital that you establish whether any overpayment has been made to the deceased. If this is the case, repayment should be made. You should always seek confirmation in writing from the Department that there are no outstanding liabilities before proceeding with the administration.

Inland Revenue
Affidavit/
Schedule of Assets

The Inland Revenue Affidavit (or schedule of assets) is a sworn declaration which details the assets of the Testator, wherever located, valued as of the date of death. It also details the debts due at the date of death and the amount of funeral expenses, thus arriving at the net value of the Estate. Details of assets passing outside the Will or on Intestacy, and details of the beneficiaries and values of the benefits are also included. The Grant of Probate cannot issue until the Inland Revenue Affidavit has been lodged and certified by the Revenue Commissioners.

Details of whether the beneficiaries have received any other gifts or inheritances either from the Testator or from any other person, on or after a specific date, must also be returned on the Affidavit. The Affidavit must be lodged with the Capital Taxes Branch of the Revenue Commissioners together with payment of Probate Tax. This information will be compared with the Inheritance Tax Returns (subsequently lodged in relation to the tax arising on individual benefits) and also with Income Tax returns filed by the deceased prior to death. The Capital Taxes Office, having examined the Affidavit, will certify it subject to the correct amount of Probate Tax having been paid.

Inland Revenue Affidavit / Schedule of Assets

Probate Tax

Probate Tax is payable by the Executor to the Revenue Commissioners at the Capital Taxes Office on the entire net value of the Estate, where that net value is above a certain threshold. With respect to Probate Tax, it is important to remember:

- This tax must be paid within nine months of the date of death (if you pay it earlier a discount is available).
- The Executor is responsible for paying the tax.
- There are a number of exemptions and reliefs available, for example, assets transferred to a surviving spouse and property held in joint names are both exempt.
- The tax is collected by self assessment and the one page return is usually filed with a cheque discharging the appropriate amount at the same time as the Inland Revenue Affidavit.

Corrective Affidavit

In certain circumstances, it is necessary to lodge a "Corrective Affidavit" with the Capital Taxes Branch at a later stage in the administration. This will account for any additional assets or liabilities which you were not aware of when the original Inland Revenue Affidavit was prepared and have only come to light since.

Inland Revenue Affidavit / Schedule of Assets

Any significant variations in the original figures, many of which will have been on an estimated basis (e.g. if you were selling a house and the house price obtained far exceeds the valuation previously furnished) can also be the subject of a corrective affidavit. When lodging the Corrective Affidavit, additional Probate Tax and Probate Fees must also be discharged at that time. In some cases, a refund may be claimed if the value has been reduced.

Applying for the Grant of Probate

The Grant of Probate is a legal document issued by the Court which confirms the right of the Executor to administer the Estate. Until the Grant of Probate issues, all the assets of the Testator are frozen. This document gives comfort to holders of the Testator's assets i.e. financial institutions etc. that the assets can be validly released to the holder of the Grant. Application for the Grant can be made in either of two ways:-

1. By personal application to the Probate Office or one of the District Probate Registries , or
2. By instructing your solicitor.

Personal Application

Unless the estate is straightforward and you can be sure that neither the asset mix nor the terms of the Will will pose any problems, it is advisable to instruct a solicitor. Should you decide to make a personal application you must complete an application form which the Probate Office will send to you on request. Once you return the completed form to the Probate Office you will be given an appointment which you must attend in person. There is usually a waiting period of a number of weeks for this appointment. At the appointment you must bring full details of the Estate together with supporting documentation including the Death Certificate, the original Will, Bank Statements, Title Deeds to any property, share valuations etc.

A probate official will prepare all the necessary papers which you will then be required to sign and swear. A fee is payable in respect of each application.

Having completed the Revenue Affidavit you will then have to attend the Capital Taxes branch of the Revenue Commissioners with the Affidavit and pay the Probate Tax. Once this is done you must return one copy of the Revenue Affidavit to the Probate office together with the Probate fee. The Probate Office will then issue the Grant of Probate.

There are 14 District Probate Registries around Ireland, all controlled by County Registrars with authority to issue Grants in cases where the deceased resided in the Counties within the jurisdiction of the particular District Registry. They are authorised to accept papers by post to lead to a Grant. The Probate Office in Dublin has all Ireland jurisdiction but is prohibited from accepting such papers by post, therefore all papers must be hand delivered.

Solicitor dealing with Grant of Probate
Where a solicitor is acting on your behalf, an application can be made by him to the Probate Registry to issue the formal Grant. In addition to the Inland Revenue Affidavit, the following documents will be prepared by your Solicitor:

1. Notice of Application.
2. Original Will and Codicil (if any).
3. Engrossment of Will and Codicil.
4. Oath of Executor.
5. Death Certificate.

In addition your solicitor may be required to prepare the following documents:

1. Affidavit of due execution of Will or Codicil.
2. Affidavit of Plight and Condition.
3. Affidavit of Testamentary capacity.
4. Renunciation of Executor.
5. Resolution of Trust Corporation.
6. Miscellaneous Affidavits i.e. identity of Executor or of deceased.

When applying for the Grant it is advisable for your solicitor to request a number of Court certified copies in order to facilitate the collection of various assets of the deceased as quickly as possible. Otherwise you will have to wait for one institution to return the Grant before sending it on to the next and so on.

If the Testator owned assets in a foreign jurisdiction, it may be necessary to take out a Grant in that jurisdiction and obtain local legal and taxation advice.

Applying for the Grant of Probate

Action following Issue of Grant

The Grant of Probate, when issued, confirms the validity of the Will and your right to collect the assets as Executor. The process of noting involves sending the original Grant or a court certified copy of the Grant to all Institutions holding assets in the name of the deceased. The existence of the Grant is then noted on their records and the assets transferred into the name of the Executor or to the beneficiaries as appropriate.

Collecting in the Assets

As soon as the Grant issues, it can be sent for noting to all relevant Financial Institutions. It is important to remember when collecting in the assets that a certain liquidity position is required in the Executor's bank account so you should start the collection process with the most liquid assets to allow for cash flow.

Cash Balances

Send the Grant for noting to the relevant Financial Institutions. Request them to close the relevant accounts and forward a cheque, made payable to you as Executor, for the proceeds of the account together with all interest accrued to date of closure. It is advisable to also request a Certificate of the interest paid from date of death to date of closure of the account for Income Tax purposes.

Action following Issue of Grant

Marketable Securities

In the case of shares which are to be distributed in specie (i.e. directly transferred to the names of the beneficiaries) then the Grant for noting should be sent together with stock certificates and stock transfer forms to the Company Registrar who will then note the share register with the new ownership. If the shares are to be sold by you as Executor, the Grant (plus the Share Certificates or details of share holdings as appropriate) should be sent to the Registrar. Amended Share Certificates will then be issued to allow you to dispose of them.

Private Company Shares

In relation to Private Company Shares, the shares can be transferred to the beneficiaries or sold as the case may be, once the Grant has been noted by the company registrar.

Chattels/Jewellery

It is not necessary to note the Grant over these assets as they can be handed over to the beneficiaries or sold by you as Executor.

Savings Certificates/Savings Bonds

The Grant should be sent to the Post Office together with the Certificates or Bonds for noting in your name, as Executor, or to be transferred to the name of a beneficiary. Alternatively you may wish to encash the investments.

If this is the case the Grant should be sent to the Post Office together with the Certificates or bonds and an encashment form. Where interest is payable on a 6 monthly basis, check to ensure you will not lose interest on early encashment.

Prize Bonds

The Grant should be sent to the Prize Bonds Office together with the Bonds, for noting and re-registration in your name, as Executor, or to be transferred to the name of a beneficiary. Alternatively you may wish to encash the Bond. If this is the case, the Grant should be sent to the Prize Bonds Office together with the Bonds and an encashment form.

Payment of Debts

Taxes up to the Date of Death

A copy Grant with the Schedule of Assets should be sent to the Inspector of Taxes (via the tax adviser dealing with the Testator's tax affairs if appropriate) together with all outstanding Tax Returns. The Inspector of Taxes will then issue assessments of all outstanding Tax liabilities which should be discharged. It is advisable to seek written confirmation from the Inspector of Taxes that all outstanding Tax liabilities are discharged in full. It is important to remember that as Executor you become liable for all taxes not paid by the Testator up to the date of death. The Irish Revenue have the power to re-open the tax affairs and reassess the position of the previous ten years if necessary.

Income Tax Post Death

As Executor you are liable to make a separate return of Income and pay Income Tax at the standard rate on Income earned by the assets in the Estate (e.g. deposit interest, dividend income, rental income) during the period of administration. There is no entitlement to personal allowances or to any of the reliefs otherwise available to individual tax payers. In certain circumstances (for instance where there are a small number of beneficiaries who are resident in the State) it is possible by concessional agreement with the Revenue that the beneficiaries may be treated as succeeding to the Income from the date of death. This avoids you having to file a separate return.

Payment of Debts

Capital Gains Tax Post Death

Death of itself does not give rise to a Capital Gains Tax charge. This means that any gain accruing from the date of purchase of any asset to the date of death of the Testator will not attract a tax charge. If however you, as Executor, sell any property during an administration period, there may be a Tax Charge arising on any increase in value or gain from the date of death to the date of disposal. The distribution of property by the Executor to the beneficiaries does not give rise to a Capital Gains Tax liability.

Other Debts & Liabilities

At this stage of the administration it is appropriate to discharge all remaining debts and liabilities. These could include such things as household bills, outstanding cheques, term loans and all other borrowing arrangements that the testator had in place at the time of his death. You should not overlook the possibility of contingent liabilities such as guarantee arrangements entered into by the Testator which survive as contingent liabilities against his Estate for a period of two years.

Statutory Notice to Creditors

To protect you from the possibility of a claim arising after you have distributed the Estate in respect of a debt due by the deceased of which you had no knowledge, you may arrange to publish a Statutory Notice to Creditors which sets out a period of six weeks by which all claims against the Estate must be received.

This is provided for in Section 49 of the Succession Act and is sometimes referred to as a Section 49 Notice.

Once you publish the Notice, you are entitled as Executor to ignore any claims arising after the expiry date (although the debtor still has a right to follow the assets of the Estate into the hands of the beneficiaries). The Statutory Notice therefore operates to protect your position as Executor in relation to outstanding debts.

The publication requirement normally is two insertions with one weeks interval between them, in a national newspaper with perhaps a similar insertion in a paper circulating in the locality where the deceased resided at the date of his death.

Other Special Entitlements

The Succession Act gives the surviving spouse and children certain rights on the deceased's estate and directs that the spouse's legal right is to have priority over devises, bequests etc. in the Will and shares on intestacy. Before proceeding to distribute the estate, you should consider the legal right of the spouse and children to be provided for out of the Estate, as this can affect the terms of the Will.

Right of Surviving Spouse under the Succession Act

A spouse is entitled to claim one-third of the Testator's Estate as their legal right share if there are children and one half if there are no children. The one-third share includes any provision that was made for them under the terms of the Will. The spouse can elect to take the family home as part of the legal right share.

Where the Testator has not provided in his Will for the spouse to receive at least a one third / one half share of the estate, you have a duty as Executor to notify the spouse in writing of their right to elect to take their legal right share. The spouse must exercise his rights within six months of the receipt of the notification from you or one year from the date of the Grant, whichever is the later.

Other Special Entitlements

Right of Children under the Succession Act

Similarly, children of the Testator, including non marital and adopted children, are entitled to make a claim under the Succession Act that they have not been adequately provided for in accordance with the Testator's means. If the Court concludes that the Testator has "failed in his moral duties to make proper provision for the child in accordance with his means, whether by his Will or otherwise", the Court can order such provision for the child out of the Testator's Estate as it thinks just. An Application must be made by the child within six months from the date of issue of the Grant.

Right of Separated Spouse or Former Spouse

Even where inheritance rights are extinguished following divorce or judicial separation proceedings, a residual right continues to vest in the surviving spouse to apply for a share of a deceased's estate on the deceased's death.

This residual right exists UNLESS, on the granting of the Decree of Separation or Divorce or any time thereafter, the Court orders that either or both spouses shall not on the death of either of them be entitled to apply for provision out of the other's estate - this is known as a "Blocking Order". This Order effectively allows the court to bar any claim being made on death.

Other Special Entitlements

As executor you must make a reasonable attempt to ensure that notice of the death is given to the separated spouse or former spouse at the earliest possible time.

The separated or former spouse must make an application to court for provision out of the deceased spouses estate within six months of the date of issue of the Grant of Probate.

To ensure that no claim can be made by the surviving spouse or that no complication arises if a claim is made after the Estate is distributed, it is advisable to wait until six months have elapsed since the issue of the Grant before distributing the Estate.

In the case of former spouses who have remarried, the court cannot make an Order for relief in their favour.

Distributing
the Estate

Before you begin to distribute the net Estate, you should be able to answer "Yes" to all the questions asked on the following Check List: ✔

- Have all debts and liabilities now been discharged? ☐
- Has the required period elapsed after issue of the Statutory Notice to Creditors? ☐
- Has the surviving spouse confirmed his intention to exercise the legal right share, if appropriate? ☐
- Are you satisfied that the Will is not to be contested by the children of the Testator? ☐
- Has clearance issued from the Department of Social Community and Family Affairs with regard to Social Welfare benefits? ☐
- Have Tax Clearance Certificates issued in respect of Capital Gains Tax, Income Tax and Inheritance Tax? ☐

"Executor's Year"

It is generally accepted that you have one year from date of death to complete the administration of an Estate. In practice many administrations for one reason or another, not always through the fault of the Executor, cannot be completed within this time. Even where there is some risk of abatement in the estate, you should consider a part payment to the beneficiaries as soon as possible.

Distributing the Estate

In general, balances should not be built up in the Executor's account in excess of what will be required to provide for all outstanding liabilities.

Solicitors and other Professional Costs

At some point nearing the end of an administration the Solicitor concerned should be asked to submit his account, including any matters which he still has to deal with. At the outset, you should have negotiated an acceptable fee structure and the only matter for resolution as this stage would be any extra costs which have been incurred due to complications not previously anticipated.

In large Estates or where the administration seems likely to be prolonged it is not unusual for the Solicitor to ask for payment on account. There is usually no reason why this should not be done, provided the payment made is well within the eventual likely total.

Care should be taken before proceeding to the final distribution of an Estate that any other professional costs (e.g. tax adviser and valuers) have been ascertained and discharged. This would include fees due to any tax adviser in respect of Income Tax which may have arisen during the course of the administration of the Estate.

Receipts

You should obtain signed receipts from the beneficiaries for distributions made or assets transferred. Such receipts should include a form of discharge to the effect that the beneficiary has received their due entitlement under the Will. If you are in any doubt as to the wording of the receipt you should consult your Solicitor for advice.

Finalising the Inheritance Tax Position

Before you distribute the assets, it is important to note that the beneficiaries are potentially liable to Inheritance Tax on the benefits taken under the Will. If the beneficiaries are liable, you as Executor are secondarily liable for any such Tax. This, in effect, means that if the beneficiaries do not pay, the Revenue Commissioners are entitled to pursue you personally for the tax. Consequently, it is advisable that all distributions made to beneficiaries are made net of tax and all tax is fully discharged by you, as Executor, on behalf of the beneficiaries. The Revenue Commissioners will then issue Certificates of Tax Clearance which allows you to go ahead and make the payments to the beneficiaries in the knowledge that all taxes are paid.

Specific Bequests

Bequests of items which do not require formal evidence of transfer (e.g. furniture, jewellery, cars) can now be handed over except where the beneficiary is a minor, in which case, the items must be retained until the minor comes of age unless there is a provision in the Will to allow the bequest to be paid to the minor's guardian. Problems sometimes arise when a beneficiary is abroad. Occasionally they may not want the bequest sent to them or alternatively, the cost of forwarding the items could be prohibitive. In these cases the beneficiary may ask for the item to be sold and the proceeds remitted to them or they may arrange for a friend or relative to store the items for them. You can agree to this if you wish but remember that the costs for the person receiving the item is a charge against the legatee.

Marketable Securities

Specific bequests of marketable securities (which are relatively rare) can be dealt with, with little difficulty, after the Grant has been noted. Remember the legatee is entitled to an apportionment of Income from the securities from the date of death unless the Will provides otherwise.

Private Company Shares

In the case of Private Companies, the Directors are not compelled to register new members and if they refuse to register the shares in the name of the beneficiary the only course open to the Executor, apart from disposing of the shares to an existing or other acceptable holder, is to approach the Company to purchase the shares themselves and to remit the proceeds to the beneficiary.

Houses and Lands

Houses and lands are vested in beneficiaries by completion of a formal Deed of Assent and your solicitor should prepare this for execution by you. The Deed of Assent should then be registered and subsequently delivered to the beneficiary with the existing Title Documents.

Charitable Donations and Bequests

The solicitor applying for the Grant of Probate should lodge a summary form with the Probate Office supplying details of any charitable bequests. This discharges you from any obligation to notify the Charitable Commissioners so you can simply pay out the cash sums to the various charities at this stage. If a bequest is made to a charity that is no longer in existence at the date of death, application could be made to the charitable commissioners to apply it to an alternative charity.

Payment of Cash Legacies

Depending on the size of the Estate and the nature of the liabilities, it may be advisable to postpone all or part of the payment of cash legacies until after the expiry date of the statutory notice to creditors (S.49 notice). If, however, you as Executor are satisfied that there are ample funds within the estate, then consideration can be given to the payment of interim cash distributions to persons entitled to cash legacies.

Distributing the Estate

After all debts of the Estate have been discharged and the S49 expiry date has passed, all cash legacies should be paid in full (net of Inheritance Tax).

In Specie and Interim Distributions to Residuary Legatees

In the interests of efficiency you should aim to make the maximum distribution to the Residuary Legatees as early as possible after the issue of the Grant. However you must retain sufficient assets, in the form of either cash or marketable securities, to meet the estimated outlay required to complete the administration. This would include funds to pay legal, accountancy and taxation fees. It is always advisable to retain somewhat more cash or shares than you require just in case some unexpected costs arise.

Care should be taken not to over distribute since beneficiaries are not under any legal obligation to refund or retransfer any distribution made to them. Careful consideration and judgement are therefore required when deciding on the amount of any interim distributions.

In Specie Distributions of Shares

Where shares are being transferred directly to a beneficiary (In Specie) and there is doubt as to whether, after such a transfer, you will have sufficient cash to provide for all liabilities of the Estate, you should consider retaining part of the shareholding(s) until all liabilities have been determined. You can then sell a sufficient number of shares to provide for any "shortfalls" and transfer the balance to the beneficiary or, if no such situation arises the entire shareholding(s) can be transferred to the beneficiary concerned.

Where there are a number of Residuary Legatees, the courses open as regards In Specie distributions are probably limited to:

(1) Selling everything and distributing in cash, or
(2) Dividing each individual holding proportionately among the beneficiaries in so far as this will give "viable" holdings and selling the remainder and distributing in cash as before. However, this option can cause difficulties because:

 (a) It is not always possible to allot stocks equitably due to the different circumstances of each stock and fluctuating values and
 (b) Varying Capital Gains Tax in relation to different holdings and different beneficiaries adds a further complication.

It is good practice, when distributing stocks, to advise beneficiaries to obtain independent advice on the above options before agreeing with them how to deal with their shareholdings.

Interim and Final Distributions to Residuary Legatees

The residue may contain items such as the family home, furniture, jewellery, car and investment properties. You as Executor have the right to appropriate some or all of these assets (subject to the right of the surviving spouse etc.) to the Residuary beneficiaries in satisfaction of their share of the residue. In practice, it is advisable to consult and agree with all the Residuary beneficiaries how you intend to carry this out.

Final Accounts

One of your last duties as Executor is to prepare a set of Administration Accounts for distribution to the Residuary beneficiaries for approval.

The final statement of Accounts can be completed once the following have been attended to:-

1. All the assets have been collected and brought under control of the Executors.
2. The expiry date of the Statutory Notice to Creditors has passed and all known debts and funeral expenses have been discharged.
3. Certificates of Discharge from CAT and CGT have been obtained and any other tax has been discharged i.e. Income Tax and Probate Tax.
4. All professional fees (Solicitors, Accountants, Valuers etc. have been discharged).
5. All pecuniary legacies have been paid and all specific bequests transferred or assented to.
6. All distributions to Residuary Legatees have been discharged.

A set of Administration accounts should include a break-down of the following headings:-
- Gross Assets
- Income Received
- Debts & Funeral Expenses
- Legacies
- Administration Expenses
- Balance for distribution to Residuary Legatees

Final Accounts

It is usual to retain a small cash balance until the statement has been completed. Any underpayments in respect of fees or other liabilities which come to light in the course of the preparation of the accounts can then be met.

In any Estate where the administration has not been completed within 12 months from the date of death, an Interim Statement should be prepared at that time and furnished to the Residuary Legatees. This practice should be repeated at the end of each subsequent year until the administration has been completed. Accounts should also be furnished to the Trustees, where the Residue is retained in Trust and will show the composition of the Residuary Trust Fund.

Residuary Trust Funds

In some cases, the Residue may not be immediately paid out, but may be held on trust in order that an income can be drawn down from it and paid to the beneficiary (usually the spouse of the deceased) for life, with the remainder to children or other parties as may be set out in the Will. In these circumstances your final responsibility as Executor is to deliver the assets going into trust together with the final statement of accounts to the Trustees. To conclude the handover of trust assets from you to the Trustees, an assent should be done vesting all the property in the Trustees. The administration of the Estate is then complete and the administration of the Trust commences.

The Steps of Administration - Check List

1. Examine the Will	
2. Meet with the beneficiaries	
3. Identify and value assets and liabilities of the deceased	
4. Protect the assets of the estate through the course of administration	
5. Prepare Inland Revenue Affidavit and submit to Revenue Commissioners	
6. Lodge papers for Grant of Probate	
7. Grant issues	
8. Collect assets	
9. Discharge liabilities	
10. Identify and discharge tax liabilities	
11. Distribute assets	
12. Discharge administration costs	
13. Prepare accounts	

Final Accounts

SECTION TWO

A Practical Guide to the Administration of Trusts

Our aim in this section of the book is to equip a lay Trustee with a sound understanding of their role. The Trustee role is extremely onerous and demanding and it is important that any person contemplating taking up the role has a full understanding of the nature of the duties and powers and the manner in which they should be exercised. Very often it is advisable that a professional Trustee will be appointed to act alongside a lay Trustee to ensure that all obligations, legal and otherwise, are fulfilled.

The Role of the Trustee

Anyone can be appointed a Trustee, including a minor or a person of unsound mind but because of the onerous duties of the office and the expertise required, it is extremely important that the persons appointed have the capacity and time to efficiently and effectively carry out their duties. Normally, it is recommended that a close family friend or relation (but not a beneficiary who may have a conflict of interest) will act together with a professional adviser or professional Trust Corporation (such as a Bank) to provide the right combination of continuity, professionalism and insight.

If you have been appointed a Trustee, you should be aware that you are obliged to act only in the best interest of the beneficiaries of the Trust and protect their entitlements by safeguarding the assets of the Trust. Before making up your mind as to whether you are going to accept your appointment as Trustee, you should acquaint yourself with what a Trust is and exactly what you, as Trustee, will have to do.

What is a Trust?

What is a Trust?

Dating from the time of the crusades, the trust is the oldest, the most enduring and one of the most flexible and useful creations of the Common Law. Simply put, a Trust involves giving legal ownership of assets to Trustees whose job is to manage them for the ultimate enjoyment of the beneficiaries. A Trust Deed sets out the intention of the person making the Trust as to who should benefit from the trust. The Deed should also set out the terms and conditions governing the trust and the powers given to the Trustees.

In general the terms of the Deed will provide either:

- That the Trustees will hold the Trust Property for the benefit of beneficiaries who have a fixed entitlement to the income or the capital of the Trust.

An example here would be a Life Interest Trust where the beneficiary/beneficiaries (life tenant) are entitled to the income generated by the Trust Assets held on trust for their lifetime, while the capital is preserved for distribution to other beneficiaries after a stipulated event occurs (usually after the death of the life tenant)

or

- That the Trustees will hold the trust property for a class of beneficiaries who have no fixed entitlement to either income or capital but merely a hope of benefiting at the Trustees discretion.

A typical example would be where a testator has provided in his Will that in the event of his dying while his children are young, his assets will be held on Discretionary Trust for the benefit of one or more of the children. The Trustees can then exercise their discretion in deciding how, in what proportions, and to which beneficiaries to distribute the funds, depending on the circumstances at that time. Under this arrangement, the children of the testator have no fixed entitlement to benefit from the Trust Funds but merely have a right to be favourably considered for a distribution.

Other examples where Trusts are used include:

Passing on a Business:
A person who has assets tied up in a business may place their shares in Trust on their death. This situation may arise where the person wishes to defer a decision as to who is to assume control of the shares and when they will do so. This is common where children are young and/or untried in business at the time of the Settlor's death.

Non-domiciled Beneficiaries:
A Trust set up to benefit non-resident beneficiaries offers significant scope to save Inheritance Tax under current legislation by liquidating a specified part of one's estate after death and investing in exempt Government Gilts for a required period of time. The Gilts can then be distributed free of Inheritance Tax to those beneficiaries who live permanently outside of Ireland.

Beneficiaries with special needs:

A trust is a useful mechanism to safeguard assets and to protect beneficiaries who need special care. These beneficiaries may include people with a longterm illness or handicap, an individual with an alcohol or drug dependency or an individual who may be in danger of exploitation by third parties. In these and other circumstances, a Trust can help protect the interests of the beneficiaries.

Concern over possible future marital break-up:

A Trust can protect assets from being dissipated outside the core family. Assets preserved on trust cannot be taken into account in a possible settlement of one the intended beneficiaries provided he is given only a potential interest to the trust assets.

Duties of Trustees

Certain duties are imposed by law on the Trustee subject to any contrary provisions in the Trust Deed. It is vital, therefore, that you first refer to the terms of the Trust Deed as this may impose additional or less onerous duties on you. You should then acquaint yourself with the duties imposed by law:-

1. *Duty to collect in Trust Property*

   As Trustee you should ensure that all of the Trust property is under your control by ensuring the property is in your name and custody. This should be done promptly and you should maintain control over the assets throughout your term of office.

2. *Duty to invest*

   You have a duty to invest the Trust Funds in order to preserve the value for the beneficiaries.

3. *Duty not to profit from the Trust*

   You are prohibited from making any profit from the Trust (unless the Trust Deed specifies otherwise) and accordingly you are not entitled to be paid for acting as Trustee irrespective of the amount of time you spend in carrying out your duties.

4. *Duty not to mix a Fund*

   As Trustee, you cannot mix the Trust Fund with either your own personal funds or with any other Trust Funds.

5. *Duty not to delegate*

   As Trustee, you cannot delegate your powers although provided the Trust Deed permits, you may delegate for the purposes of administration to professionals, i.e. solicitors, bankers, tax advisers and property agents.

6. *Duty to distribute*

   You must, as Trustee, distribute the income and capital of the Fund as the Trust Deed instructs.

7. *Duty to maintain equality between the beneficiaries*

   It is imperative that you as Trustee act with fairness and integrity.

8. *Duty to provide Accounts and Information*

   You must, as Trustee, keep accounts of all dealings in Trust property and be able to furnish a full record to the beneficiaries.

Duties of Trustees

Powers of Trustees

There are two main sources of Trustees powers:

- Powers given under the General Law
- Powers given by the Trust Deed

If the Trust deed does not have a specific power, then you do not have it unless there is a provision under General Law.
The principal piece of Trust legislation in Ireland is the Trustee Act 1893, and Part II of this Act sets out various powers and duties of Trustees.

Power of Sale

As Trustee, you are permitted to sell depreciating property. Generally, if the assets are wasting, hazardous or unauthorised investments which involve risk to capital, you are obliged to sell.

Power to Give Receipts

As Trustee you have power to issue a receipt in writing in respect of Trust property sold or transferred and that receipt will act as a discharge to the purchaser. Unless the Trust deed expressly authorises it, a Sole Trustee cannot give a valid receipt for the proceeds of sale.

Power to Insure Buildings

As Trustee, you are authorised to effect insurance in respect of Trust property although the amount of insurance cover is not to exceed 75% of the value of the property. If you wish to insure more than 75% of the value of the property, you will need an express power in the Trust Deed to allow you to do so.

Power to Renew Leases

Trustees are empowered to renew any leases of Trust property.

Power to Compound Liabilities

As Trustee, you have power to accept a compromise of a debt or decide not to pursue a debt and you may act to settle disputes in relation to Trust properties without being responsible for any loss, provided you act in good faith.

Power to Delegate

You are empowered to delegate your duties for the purposes of administration but not for decisions on policy nor for exercise of discretionary powers. You can delegate duties in cases where you require professional assistance (for example from lawyers, tax advisers, valuers or bankers).

Power of Advancement

As Trustee, you may make capital available to minor beneficiaries.

It is clear from the above that the requirements for acting as Trustee are continuity, objectivity, impartiality, know-how and capacity and time. In our experience, these are best found by including a professional Trustee. This can be done by appointing a professional at the outset when the Trust Deed is being drawn up or, by adding the professional Trustee under a deed of appointment or by substituting under a Deed of Retirement and Execution.

Trust Administration

Reading a Trust Deed

Your first action as Trustee is to familiarise yourself with the terms of the trust deed and to satisfy yourself that the Trust is legally valid. In some cases the terms of the Trust Deed may not be clear and easy to follow. In construing or interpreting the Trust Deed, the following are useful guidelines.

- Seek to ascertain the intention of the person creating the trust.
- What is the meaning of what is said - not what did he mean to say.
- Try and construe the document on the day of its execution.
- It is necessary to construe documents as a whole rather than focus on specific portions of the document in isolation to the rest of the document.
- Insofar as is possible, words and phrases should be given their ordinary and plain meaning - except that legal or technical words and phrases should be given their legal or technical meaning.

To be certain that you as Trustee understand the legal formalities of the trust structure, it is advisable to take legal advice from a Solicitor.

The "Contract" for such advice should be fully understood by both you and your solicitor. It should clearly set out whether the advice is transaction specific or on a retainer basis. In the latter case, the solicitor would advise generally concerning developments that may arise from time to time over the lifetime of the trust. You should also confirm at this time whether this contract covers tax advice. You should agree the fee structure with the solicitor at the outset and this should then be confirmed in writing to you.

Requirements for a Valid Trust

To be certain a Valid Trust has been created there are a number of legal principles to be satisfied:

(A) Three Certainties:

1. Certainty of Subject matter:
Is the property, which is the subject matter of the Trust, clearly defined.

2. Certainty of intention:
Is the wording used to create the Trust clear and unambiguous?

3. Certainty of Object:
Are the people to benefit i.e. the beneficiaries, clearly defined?

(B) Is the Vesting Date - (Finishing Date) clear?

It is not possible to put property into trust forever (unless it is a Charitable trust). Every trust has a term, or as it is alternatively known a "perpetuity" period.

The "Rule against Perpetuities" is a complex formula which prevents property in Ireland being tied up indefinitely. It provides that every Trust must vest or terminate after a period comprising the life, or lives, in being of individuals named in the Trust Instrument plus twenty one years. If this rule is breached the Trust can fail. In practice, Trusts can endure in this way for up to 100 years.

(C) Have all the Statutory formalities being complied with?
Will Trusts must satisfy the requirements of the Succession Act 1965. Trusts comprising Real Property must satisfy the Statute of Frauds Act 1865.

Collecting in the Trust Property

A Trustee must arrange for all the Trust Assets to be put into their name as Trustee and ensure that they are under their full control.

In the case that you are being appointed as a new Trustee to an existing Trust, it is advisable at the outset to have a meeting with the retiring Trustees.

The agenda for the meeting should include:

- Details of all Trust Assets
- Full history of the Trust and its beneficiaries
- Details of any actual or threatened trust litigation

Trust Administration

You can confirm what assets are held in the Trust by examining:-

- The Trust Accounts for the previous six years- (if the appointment is in relation to an existing trust).
- The final Administration Accounts - (if the appointment is to a trust arising out of a Will).

If the Trust Assets include Real Property, this needs to be specifically conveyed or assigned to you as new Trustee. Stocks and Shares need to be registered in your name as Trustee, and Share Certificates delivered to you. A full inventory of all chattels in trust needs to be compiled and you should satisfy yourself that they are held securely and adequately, in custody, and also insured.

If the Trust Assets includes cash, then you should notify the relevant financial institution that you are the new Trustee so that the Account can be transferred to your name and new Mandates completed. The Financial Institution(s) will most probably require sight of the Trust Deed as proof of your status. In the event that you cannot take control of a Trust Asset, (for example, where a retiring Trustee refuses to hand over a trust asset) it may be necessary to go to Court for directions as to whether proceedings should be instituted to recover the asset.

Having made sure that all the Trust Assets are now registered in your name, you should seek to obtain all relevant documentation including all legal documentation, Counsels opinions, details of any Court actions, Trust files and records from the retiring Trustees together with a full account from them of any potential difficulties.

Trust Records

A significant area of risk for you as Trustee is failure to keep proper records. While you will never intend to act negligently or in breach of trust, your actions may be capable of misinterpretation. Without proper records evidencing the way in which you have conducted the affairs of the trust, you may find yourself liable to the beneficiaries, and to the Trust in general, on grounds of Maladministration and/or Breach of Trust. To ensure that you are seen to keep proper records, it is advisable to organise the Trust Records as follows:

Correspondence File

Your correspondence file should contain routine correspondence relating to the affairs of the Trust filed in chronological order. It is important that current letters are not filed away until a satisfactory response has been received or given. You will need to ensure that you actively follow up each issue; it will not be acceptable to excuse any delay due to a delayed response by other third parties.

During the term of the Trust there are key events which will affect the way you deal with the Trust Assets. You should carefully record your response to and awareness of these events.

Examples include:

- A birth which may represent an addition to the class of beneficiaries which under the terms of the Trust may result in a reduction of the shares of the existing beneficiaries.
- The marriage of a beneficiary which may result in the spouse becoming entitled to a share of the Trust Income and/or Capital or conversely the original beneficiary's interest ceasing.
- The divorce of a beneficiary and/or subsequent remarriage and its effect on the beneficiary class.
- The death of the person entitled to the Trust Income resulting in the Trust becoming payable to the entitled beneficiaries.
- The death of a co-Trustee which may require a new Trustee to be appointed.
- A beneficiary attaining a specified age signalling that no one else is entitled to be a beneficiary.

While the above may be regarded as once-off events, other matters of a more routine nature also require to be detailed in the Trust records.

Examples include:

- Changes of address of beneficiaries, Trustees Agents or other Advisers
- Changes in beneficiaries' Bankers
- Alterations in the Trustee investment holdings such as purchases and sales
- Changes in a Private Company's name
- Alterations in a Private Company's share capital, bonus and rights issues etc
- Take-overs, mergers and buyouts in Private Company shares

Permanent Documents File:

The Permanent Documents File should contain copies of all Deeds and other important documents and items of correspondence which will have continuing relevance during the existence of the Trust. These would include:

- Trust Deeds, Court Orders, Trustees Declarations and Settlors Letters of Wishes
- Counsel's Opinions
- Details of the location of Title Documents
- Record of exercise of discretionary powers
- Confirmation of Tax Status from the Revenue (if appropriate)
- Beneficiaries' Marriage Certificates, Death Certificates, Birth Certificates

Financial File:

This should contain the following two folders:-

1) Investment Folder

All documentation and correspondence with regard to the purchase, sale and transfer of investments should be filed here. These should include valuations, contracts and broker statements. Minutes of all meetings recording consideration of the Trusts investments and performance of same should also be on this file. The file can then act as your central investment record which is available when queries on a Trust's investment history arise. Remember that remaindermen of the trust may pose these queries many years after events have occurred.

2) Taxation Folder

The taxation folder should contain:
- Copies of Tax Returns including a photocopy of the completed and signed Tax Return for each year.
- Tax computations and supporting schedules.
- Notices of Assessments together with copies of appeals, postponement applications and receipts for tax paid.
- Tax correspondence.

Taxation

It is important, at the start of your role as Trustee, to establish who is liable for all the relevant taxes.

Income Tax

As Trustee, you will be assessed for Income Tax and must file Income Tax returns in respect of trust income. This is quite separate to your own personal Income Tax position. Trust income is liable to Income Tax at the standard rate of tax but you will not be able to claim any of the normal personal allowances/reliefs available to individuals. In computing Income Tax you are not allowed to deduct expenses of administration of the trust. You may arrange for part or all of the trust income to be paid directly from its source to the beneficiary. In such circumstances the Income Tax liability is the responsibility of the beneficiary - not of you as Trustee. However, the Revenue must be informed of the name and address of the beneficiary and the Income received by the beneficiary.

Generally where payments are paid out of income, they will be taxed as income and Payments made out of Accumulated income will be treated as Capital Appointments. If income of a Trust has not been distributed within 18 months of the end of the year of assessment in which it arises, it will be subject to a surcharge of 20%. In calculating the surcharge, you can deduct trust administrative expenses.

Capital Gains Tax

When a person creates a Trust, the transfer of the assets into the trust is a deemed disposal for CGT purposes and that person must pay CGT on any gains.

There are two types of disposals which make you potentially liable to CGT as Trustee:

Actual Disposal

If you dispose of assets in the course of administering the trust, you will be liable to pay CGT on any gains made. Deductions can be claimed for the normal acquisition, disposal and enhancement costs. You cannot claim the annual exemption and other individual reliefs except for principal private residence relief made on the disposal of a dwelling which was "the only or main residence" of an individual entitled to occupy it under the terms of the Trust.

Deemed Disposal

You will be deemed to have disposed of assets:-

(a) When a person becomes absolutely entitled to the trust asset (for example, if an asset is held on trust for a minor until they reach age 18, that individual becomes absolutely entitled to the asset on reaching age 18). In this case you will be deemed to dispose of the asset and immediately reacquire it at its market value, which will then be the base cost for the beneficiary should they decide to sell it.

(b) On the death of a life tenant and where the trust assets continue to be held in trust.

Capital Acquisitions Tax

Capital Acquisitions Tax (CAT) is a tax on gifts and inheritances. Each beneficiary has a Tax Free threshold up to which no CAT is payable. Once this threshold is reached, CAT will be levied. The Tax Free threshold is determined by the relationship between the donor and the recipient.

The person in receipt of the Gift or Inheritance is the person primarily liable to pay Capital Acquisitions Tax. However, as Trustee you have a secondary liability. Secondary liability is limited to the value of the property and the Income from same.

If you pay the CAT, as Trustee, you may recover the amount paid from the person primarily accountable. The one exception in reclaiming the tax paid from a beneficiary is where you have discharged the CAT liability of a Life Tenant. As Trustee you cannot recover the amount paid from the life tenant. Instead the Trust Fund is reduced by the CAT liability so that in effect the Life Tenant indirectly bears the tax, year by year, as a result of the reduced Annual Trust Income. In practical terms, it is advisable, in the case of cash benefits to pay the CAT on behalf of the beneficiary and to pay the net amount directly to the beneficiary. However, when the benefit comprises shares or land, it is advisable to ensure that the CAT has been discharged either directly by the beneficiary or by you, on receipt of funds from the beneficiary, before transferring the shares or land into the beneficiary's name.

It is vital for you to protect yourself against any CAT liability by refraining from making any distribution pending receipt of a Clearance Certificate from the Revenue Commissioners.

Discretionary Trust Taxes

If you are a Trustee of a Discretionary Trust you will be liable to additional taxes as follows:-

1. A once-off discretionary trust levy of 6% (subject to a 3% refund in certain circumstances) of the value of the assets held in trust and
2. A 1% annual charge on the value of the assets held in trust on 5th April of each year.

<u>The 6% levy becomes payable on the later of the following three dates:-</u>

1. The date on which the property becomes subject to the Discretionary Trust, or
2. The date of death of the disponer, or
3. The date on which the youngest principal object attains the age of twenty-one.

    A principal object is the spouse of the disponer, the child of the disponer or the minor child of a predeceased child of the disponer.

It is important that you ensure that the tax is discharged because you as Trustee are primarily accountable for this tax. Any beneficiary of the Discretionary Trust is secondarily accountable provided he has benefited from the Trust Funds.

For the purpose of the annual levy, the Revenue will accept values of non voting shares, lands and houses agreed at one valuation date for the following two years, as it can often be expensive and time consuming to obtain values of certain Assets on an annual basis. This means that it will only be necessary to obtain valuations of such Assets every three years.

Exemption from the 6% and 1% Discretionary Trust Taxes will be granted for Discretionary Trusts created exclusively for certain purposes including: Public and Charitable Trusts, and Trusts which have been created for the benefit of one or more named individuals who are incapable of managing their own affairs because of age, improvidence or a physical, mental or legal incapacity.

Tax on Charitable Trusts

Charitable trusts are exempt from the various taxes provided the Revenue Commissioners certify them as charitable.

Table of Tax and Payment Deadlines

Type of Tax	Submit Return By	Pay Tax By
Income Tax	31st January	1st November
CGT	31st January	1st November
CAT	within 4 mths of the valuation date	within 4 mths of the valuation date
Probate Tax	within 9 mths of death	within 9 mths of death
Surcharge	5th October	5th October
6% Disc. Tax	within 4 mths of death of Settlor or 21st birthday of youngest principal object, whichever is later	within 4 mths of death of Settlor or 21st birthday of youngest principal object, whichever is later
1% Disc. Tax	by 5th August	by 5th August

Trust Accounts

You as Trustee are obliged to keep proper accounts and records and make them available to the beneficiaries for inspection. There is no obligation on you to have the accounts audited but it may be advisable to do so in the case of substantial complex trusts. As with the appointment of Solicitors for the trust, it is important for you to enter into a "contract" with tax advisers for the trust. This should clearly set out the work which will be done by the tax advisers. The need for ongoing financial/tax advice during the lifetime of the Trust cannot be emphasised sufficiently. You should agree, in consultation with the tax advisers, the format of the accounts and the level of information required.

Ideally beneficiaries should have access to the following information:

Details of the Trust:

- Who created the Trust?
  - The circumstances under which the trust came into existence (i.e. on the execution of a deed or on the death of the Testator).
  - The date on which the Trust was created or the Testator died
  - A summary of the terms in the original Deed creating the Trust which govern:
- who is to benefit and the nature of the benefit.
- Distribution and/or the accumulation of the Income.
- A summary of the Terms of each Deed which affects the terms of the Trust which would include deeds of Family Arrangement or court orders.

Financial Statements

The Financial Statements should distinguish the Assets held as Capital and those representing Income and associated liabilities.

The financial information can be further separated out as follows:

Capital Account
The following assets should be shown separately
- Cash balances representing assets held on trust
- Cash balances representing assets held for immediate distribution to the beneficiaries

Income Account
The following Assets should be shown separately
- Income balances to which beneficiaries are immediately entitled
- Income which may be distributed or accumulated at the discretion of the Trustees
- Income charged with the payment of a particular obligation such as amended arrangements after divorce or where the Income stream is used as security for borrowings

Liabilities
The following should be shown separately
- Liabilities to: Income Tax, Capital Gains Tax, Inheritance Tax, Discretionary Trust Levies

- Outstanding accruals, including accruals for Trustees expenses and costs
- Liabilities, the repayment of which is to be made only out of the proceeds of sale of the particular Assets
- Liabilities other than in £IR/Euro should appear expressed in the accounts both in the original currency and as translated to the £IR or Euro at the rate of exchange on the appropriate date

Assets

If the Book Value of the Assets in the financial statements is other than their original cost, describe the basis for the new valuation (i.e. the probate value, or re-evalued as of a certain date)

Categorise the Assets in the financial statements as follows:

- Assets to be held for an indefinite period, which comprise the body of the Trust Assets.

  These should be grouped in the following broad classifications:-

    - Freehold land and buildings
    - Leasehold land and buildings
    - Plant machinery and motor vehicles

- Chattels
- Unlisted Investments
- Listed Investments-the total market value at the close of business on the nearest business days of listed investments should appear against these investments.
- Loans to third parties
- Loans to beneficiaries
- Bank balances, showing separately balances on
    - Current Accounts
    - Deposit Accounts
    - Special or fixed term Deposit Accounts
- Cash
- Assets held to pay current liabilities and accruals
- Assets held for immediate distribution to beneficiaries
  Unless they are disclosed in separate accounts, it is advisable to distinguish Assets held specifically for particular beneficiaries.

If there are co-Trustees, then you should arrange for each co-Trustee to approve and sign the accounts.

Providing Information to Beneficiaries

Beneficiaries are entitled to a level of information that will allow them and their Advisers to reasonably assess that you as Trustee have discharged your duties in an honest, cost effective and efficient manner.

It is well established that beneficiaries have proprietary rights to certain information forming part of the Trust records. In this context the Courts have made it plain that the following documents may be disclosed to beneficiaries:

- Advice from Counsel and Solicitors to the Trustees
- All Deeds
- Annual Trust Accounts
- Financial data such as the balance sheet and profit and loss accounts of companies in which Trustees are invested
- Investment advice received by Trustees
- Correspondence with investment Advisers including Surveyors, Valuers etc.
- Details of rent arrangements regarding land
- Copies of Income and Expenditure Accounts relating to properties
- Tax returns and correspondence with the Revenue Commissioners, Capital Taxes Office etc.

- Subsidiary documents such as a Letter of Wishes, if not expressly or impliedly confidential.
- Correspondence between the Settlor and Trustees if not expressly or implicitly confidential.

In general every effort should be made by you to facilitate beneficiaries with access to information. There is nothing more likely to cause suspicion and distrust than apparent evasiveness on your part.

Trustees Remuneration

The general rule is that you are not permitted to receive payment for acting as Trustee. There are however certain permitted exceptions to this general principle.

- If there is a "charging clause" in the Trust Instrument, then you can be paid accordingly.
- Even if there is no charging clause, its possible for a Solicitor/Trustee to charge his professional fees for work he does on behalf of himself and one or more co-Trustees in connection with legal proceedings brought by or against the Trustees.
- If all the beneficiaries are of full age and sound mind, and between them are absolutely entitled to the property, they can enter into a contract with you under which you are authorised to receive payment for acting as Trustee.
- If the Court appoints a Trust corporation, then the Court may authorise that the Trust corporation can be paid. The Court can also authorise the payment to a Trustee for doing work that is outside the normal course of events.

Trustees Expenses

Both professional and lay Trustees are entitled to be reimbursed for expenses incurred in the discharge of their functions. Such expenses would include external professional advice, travel costs, subsistence etc. In relation to the travel and subsistence costs, a good rule of thumb is always the amounts or allowances published by the Revenue Commissioners for use by Public Servants.

Trustees Meetings

If the Trust is an active one with a wide variety of Trust Assets and an extensive beneficiary class, it may be necessary to have more than one meeting a year. The complexity of the Assets held in Trust and what's happening in the Trust at any one time, largely dictate the frequency with which the Trustees should meet. At a minimum, if there is more than one Trustee, you should meet at least once a year. The annual meeting should include a full review of all matters relating to the Trust including:-

- Formal review of investment performance
- Review of Trust Accounts / Valuations
- Update on beneficiaries situations

Probably the most important function of the Trustees meeting is the exercising of the Trustees discretion in relation to the appointment out of the Capital or Income of a Trust. It is entirely up to you as Trustee to decide how you wish to formally record the exercise of your discretion.

If the exercise of your discretion is subsequently challenged in Court proceedings, you may be obliged to produce the record of your deliberations and also you may be challenged that you allowed undue /improper influence e.g. that you were effectively acting at the discretion of a particular beneficiary. It is well established that you cannot be challenged over how you ultimately exercised your discretion, unless you did this in bad faith or negligently. You can, however, be challenged on the basis that you did not consider all the relevant facts, including the circumstances of all the beneficiaries. This places a considerable onus on you when exercising your discretion as the Trust records need to provide a level of detail which you may not have anticipated.

Investment of Trust Assets

As Trustee, you have a general duty to invest Trust Property, taking into account the interests of all the various beneficiaries. Where one person is entitled to the Income for their lifetime, this person's interest in maximising the Income return must be matched against the interest of the other beneficiaries in the Capital Appreciation of the Trust Assets.

In addition to your duty to invest the Trust Property, you have a further duty to invest in Trustee Authorised Investments or within the terms of the Trust Deed. In making investment decisions you must exercise Ordinary Prudence in your decision making. Ordinary Prudence is defined as acting as a reasonable man when making investment decisions.

You should take account of the following:-

Does the Trust Deed give you power to Invest in all Types of Investments?

Most modern Trust Deeds will give Trustees full powers to invest as if they themselves were the beneficial owners. Some of the older Trusts may have public policy restrictions such as a restriction on investments in the "tobacco industry" etc. One of the more common investment decisions you may have to make is whether or not to purchase a house for one or more of the beneficiaries to live in.

Ideally a well drafted Trust Deed will specifically allow you to do this, without incurring responsibility for whether or not this is a good investment decision. In the absence of such a power, you should fully consider the needs of all the beneficiaries before tying up a proportion of capital in this way.

If the Trust Deed has no investment powers, then the Trustees are restricted to Trustee Authorised Investments, which is a mix of government and top rated corporate securities, bonds and other similar "blue chip" investments.

Do You Have Power to Employ Investment Advisers?

It is usual to provide in a Trust Deed power to the Trustees to employ the services of a professional Investment Adviser, however the mere fact that you employ an Investment Adviser does not remove responsibility from you for this function. In addition to deciding on which Investment Adviser to use, it is prudent for you to agree investment objectives in advance and, more importantly, to make arrangements to monitor the performance of the Investment Adviser into the future.

Setting Investment Objectives

In deciding on investment objectives, you must consider the type of Trust that has been created and the various interests of the beneficiaries.

For example, a Trust with one individual absolutely entitled to all the Income, and another beneficiary entitled to the capital on the first individual's death, will create a need to balance the requirement for an Income stream against a requirement for capital appreciation.

In other circumstances, there may be no real need for Income in the short to medium term, but with some uncertainty as to Income needs in the long term. The investment objective should therefore be individually tailored to suit each specific Trust. In addition, you should consider existing investments which have been part of the Trust Assets when you took over as Trustee and whether or not you should retain these investments or sell them and reinvest the proceeds. At a minimum, when setting the investment objectives, you should have in mind a simple model of Asset Allocation.

Choosing an Investment Adviser

Today's climate of intensive regulation should give some comfort to you when choosing an Investment Adviser. Provided you chose an Adviser who is bonded or regulated as appropriate, you cannot be guilty of negligence in choosing them. The problem facing you is which one of the regulated bonded Advisers to appoint. One possible strategy to adopt is to ask two or more prospective Advisers to present written proposals as to how they would recommend the fund be invested (based always on your Investment objectives). The presentation of the written proposals is a very important meeting for you and the potential Advisers alike.

Given the long term nature of Trusts, it is of paramount importance that good working relationships are established from the outset. In evaluating the proposals of the Advisers, you should take account of the following:

- **How has the investment adviser approached the three basic considerations of liquidity, stability and growth?**
  For example, there is little point in establishing an investment policy which features extensive investment in roll up funds, which does not provide adequately for an ongoing Income requirement. Likewise, it would be foolish to have the whole fund in US$ if the requirements of the beneficiaries are £IR and £Stg.
- **What is the track record of the investment adviser?**
  Most written proposals should feature some comparative analysis and statistics which show how the adviser has performed vis a vis other competitors.
- **Cost as always should be a consideration**

Investment Management Agreement

Having made the decision on the appropriate appointment based on all the above (and personal preference), the next stage for you is to execute an Investment Management Agreement.

This agreement, which is entered into by you and the Investment Adviser sets out the services that will be provided, as well as the reporting arrangements (i.e. frequency and type of valuations to be furnished) and the cost of such services. It should also state in broad terms the investment objectives to be followed and any particular restrictions that the Trust Deed or you, the Trustee, wish to specify.

The agreement should also contain provisions governing the removal of the Investment Adviser, which are clearly important, (but often forgotten), as this allows you to deal efficiently with any underperformance of the Investment Adviser. To facilitate a good active and open relationship between you and the Investment Adviser, it is helpful at this time to clarify who you will be dealing with in the office of the Investment Adviser.

Monitoring Investment Performance

The obligation on you to monitor the performance of your Investment Advisers continues for the duration of the Trust. The frequency and extent of the monitoring will largely depend on the size and nature of the Trust Assets. You will have to monitor both the absolute performance of the fund in isolation and the relative performance against its peers. When agreeing the terms of the Investment Management Agreement, the requirement for frequency of valuations can be agreed. It is usual to get these quarterly but, for bigger funds, monthly valuations may be advisable. There should be at minimum an annual meeting between you and the Investment Adviser to discuss in depth the performance of the portfolio and decide on any necessary variations, taking into account the changing needs of the beneficiaries and the market itself.

In some cases it may be advisable for you to consider employing a professional to review the performance of the Investment Adviser.

Transactions in Trust Assets

From time to time you will want to enter into transactions concerning Trust Assets for example, buying and selling Trust property. There are certain fundamental questions to be answered when dealing with Trust Assets:

- Is the power to enter into the proposed transaction contained in the Trust Deed?
- What is the rationale behind the transaction?
- Is it in the interests of the beneficiaries?
- Has professional advice been obtained as to the merits of the transaction?

Based on satisfactory answers to the above, you may decide to proceed. It is important to emphasise again the necessity for you to be meticulous in your record keeping. All minutes of meetings, conversations etc., concerning the transaction, should be efficiently filed and stored.

Freehold & Leasehold Property

Acquisitions

You may invest in land as Trustee if:

(1) You are specifically empowered to do so under the terms of the Trust Deed (most modern Trust deeds contain a power permitting Trustees to invest as if they were the absolute owner of the Trust Assets, which would cover this type of investment). As previously noted, investment in Real Property does not always produce a return equivalent to other investments such as Stocks and Shares. There may, however, be very good reasons for making such an investment and you should be careful to clearly record your reasoning as to how you arrived at the decision.

(2) All the Trust beneficiaries are of full age and sound mind and authorise you to invest in land, or

(3) You are granted authority following an application to Court.

It should be noted that where land is to be purchased for the occupation of a beneficiary it is therefore not strictly an investment since it does not produce an income. In this instance different criteria may apply. For instance, it may be necessary for a specific power to be contained in the Trust Deed before land can be acquired for this purpose.

You need to understand the taxation implications of each transaction. Purchasing a house for a beneficiary in a Discretionary Trust is likely to create a tax charge arising both on the granting of occupation and on the beneficiary ceasing to occupy the property whether on his death or otherwise.

Before entering into any commitment to purchase property, you should obtain and consider a full report and valuation from a qualified independent Valuer or Surveyor. The report should include a specific recommendation as to the price which should be paid for the property given its current state and the state of the market for equivalent properties. Advice should be taken on suitable insurance cover for the acquired property and this cover should be activated when appropriate. In circumstances where a beneficiary is to occupy the property and is made responsible for effecting insurance cover and paying annual premiums, it is essential that the Insurance Company is notified of your interest in the property and requested to endorse this interest on the Policy.

The usual procedure on acquiring land is for a deposit of up to 10% to be paid on exchange of contracts, with the balance of the purchase price becoming payable on completion of the contracts This usually happens within six weeks of the exchange of contracts. On conclusion of the purchase formalities, the completed statement submitted by the Solicitors should be checked by you and arrangements made to hold the title documents for safekeeping either at the Solicitor's office or in a Bank.

Ownership

As with your own personal property, certain routine reviews are essential. Key dates relevant to investment property would include:

- The dates by which notice should be given of rent reviews
- Tenancy expiration dates
- The date on which annual review of insurance cover is undertaken
- Due dates for the receipt of Rental Accounts from Agents (if appropriate)
- Due dates for periodic inspections by Agents

In circumstances where a beneficiary occupies a Trust property, he is frequently made responsible for paying outgoings of an Income nature, such as water or sewerage rates, insurance premiums, ground rents and the cost of any repairs to the house.

Where you have a portfolio of properties administered by Agents on your behalf, you should engage the services of a tax adviser to ensure that the relevant Income and Capital Gains Tax returns are made.

Disposal

In order to fulfil your obligations to the beneficiaries, it is important that you are seen to obtain the best possible price for the property. This will normally involve seeking expert opinion on a number of issues including the property's current value, the most favourable means of disposing of it, whether by private treaty sale, sale by tender or auction and on any offers received for the property.

All offers for the property should be considered and unless there are valid reasons for deciding otherwise (such as doubts as to the financial position of the Purchaser) the highest offer should be accepted. For this reason where "gazumping" occurs, you are not always able to adopt the moral stance of an individual vendor unless you have reason to consider that any new potential purchaser does not intend to complete the transaction.

Private Company Shares

When the Trust holds shares in a Private Company, you are under an obligation to ensure that you are kept fully informed as to the Company's progress, results and prospects. At the very least you should arrange to receive the Annual Accounts and Reports.
In certain circumstances where the holding is substantial, the above information should be supplemented by monthly Management Accounts and the Agenda and Minutes of Board Meetings. You should also attend the Annual General Meeting.

It may also be advisable for you to consider having board representation by appointing a Director to high-risk businesses to represent the Trust's interests.

Attendance at AGM

In advance of attendance at a Company's AGM (and particularly if it's your only opportunity to meet and discuss the affairs of the Company with the Company's management), you should fully familiarise yourself with the financial statements circulated to the members. As a basis for fully understanding the financial position of the Company, you should have a broad understanding of what the Company produces, its strengths and weaknesses and the threats and opportunities in its environment. In the event that you are not familiar with financial statements you should consider getting a professional accountant to assess them to keep you informed and satisfy yourself on all relevant aspects of the business.

The Financial Statements circulated will generally consist of a Profit and Loss Statement, a Balance Sheet, a Cash Flow Statement and a Statement of total realised Gains and Losses. In general by the time an AGM is convened the figures as furnished are relatively historic. It is important, therefore, to be aware of the trends that will give you some indication of how the Company is expected to perform in the future. The records of the Trust should clearly indicate that you prepared yourself for the AGM and contributed to it as appropriate.

Most modern Trust Deeds (particularly those where the Trust Assets consist of shares in a family business) contain a clause absolving you from being involved in the management or conduct of the business of the Company. This clause may also expressly permit you to leave the conduct of the business (including taking decisions on whether or not to pay dividends) to the directors unless you have reason to suspect fraudulent management.

In practice it is not advisable to rely on this and do nothing. Your duty to the beneficiaries requires that you should nevertheless act with normal prudence and diligence in all matters affecting the Trusts share holding in the Company. Similar care should be taken in expressing the voting rights attaching to the shareholding with a view to maintaining independence, bearing in mind that your primary responsibilities are to the beneficiaries.

Chattels and Works of Art

Chattels and works of art are not normally classified as investments, in that they do not usually yield an Income. As a result, if you acquire and hold them, you should be specifically empowered to do so by the Trust Deed. It may happen that chattels or works of art are already included in the Trust Assets. In these circumstances it is clearly your duty to obtain and maintain an inventory of them and to ensure that they are adequately insured and kept in good condition.

You should undertake the following checks on an annual basis:

(i.) Verification of the Inventory. Make a note of any items lost, destroyed or otherwise discarded through wear and tear.
(ii.) Confirmation of Insurance cover.
(iii.) Revision of the level of insurance cover in conjunction with an approved valuer.
(iv.) That you have met your obligations under Capital Gains Tax on the disposal of the objects.

Loans

You may decide to extend loan facilities to a beneficiary of the Trust. For example, where a beneficiary has already received substantial benefits from the Trust and wishes to purchase a house - rather than make a further capital distribution you may decide to give a loan facility. In such cases documentary evidence of the loan and its terms should be obtained at the outset and signed by you and the beneficiary. In its simplest form, the documentation may consist of an acknowledgement signed by the beneficiary. For larger loans the documentation should include a Loan Agreement setting out the amount to be borrowed, the applicable interest rate and the security which may include a fixed charge on property.

Investment of Trust Assets

Appointment, Removal and Retirement of Trustees

Appointment

The first Trustees are usually appointed by the original Trust Deed. New or additional Trustees can then be appointed in accordance with the framework provided for in the Trust Deed. This power to appoint may be given to you to provide for the retirement of one of the Trustees., or can be reserved to the person creating the Trust for the duration of his lifetime and thereafter to another third party.

In addition to any express powers contained in the Trust Deed, S.10 of the Trustee Act 1893, provides for the appointment of new Trustees in certain circumstances. This power, which must be exercised in writing, may be exercised by the person or persons entitled under the Trust Deed, or the current Trustees, or the personal representatives of the last surviving Trustee.

The power can be exercised where a Trustee:

- Is dead, or
- Remains out of the jurisdiction for more than 12 months or
- Wishes to be discharged from his duties or
- Refuses to act or
- Is unfit or incapable of acting

It is important to be aware, when using this provision, that the power is confined to the appointment of *replacements* for original or substituted Trustees, and not for the addition of a Trustee, except, when a Trustee is being replaced, the number of Trustees can be increased.

Removal of Trustees

The removal of Trustees can be an emotive issue, both for the Trustees and those seeking their removal. It is a situation that requires careful handling as bad feeling can quickly escalate and substantial costs can be incurred endeavouring to find a resolution to the problems.

The actual power to remove a Trustee may be exercised under an express power in the Trust Deed. In the absence of an express power, there is a statutory power contained in S 23 of the 1893 Act, where the Court can appoint a new Trustee in place of an existing Trustee. The Court also has power to remove a Trustee (without necessarily replacing him as per S 23) where it appears necessary for the proper execution of the Trust. Trustees have an obligation to act in harmony with one another in the interests of the beneficiaries. Trustees who maintain a troublesome attitude and impede the good administration of the Trust, run the risk that costs will be awarded against them personally in any Court action taken to remove them.

Retirement of Trustees

When you accept an appointment as Trustee, it's worth noting that retiring from that Trusteeship can prove to be difficult. If there are more than two Trustees any one of you may declare in writing that you wish to be discharged. If your co-Trustees accept your wish to retire, the Trust Assets can then be transferred into the names of the continuing Trustees. If, however, there is only you and one other Trustee, a substitute or replacement Trustee must be found before one of you can retire.

If the beneficiaries of a Trust are all of full age and absolutely entitled to all the Trust property, they can effectively terminate the Trust and release the Trustee from his duties.

Glossary

Abatement	Where the estate after payment of debts, is insufficient to pay all legacies in full, each legacy will be reduced on a pro-rata basis i.e. abated.
Absolute interest	Gift taken under a Will which is unlimited and complete and covers the right to both income and capital of the asset.
Ademption	Where an asset specifically bequeathed in a Will is not in the ownership of the Testator or no longer exists at the date of death, the bequest fails and is said to be adeemed.
Administration Bond	Insurance bond that must be taken out by the personal representative of an intestate estate or where the personal representative is someone other than the executor.
Administrator	Person appointed by the Court to administer an intestate estate or where someone other than the appointed executor is administering the estate.
Advancement	Where account is taken of prior capital gifts made by the testator to his children during his lifetime in determining the children's share of the estate.
Appropriation	The satisfaction of a debt or cash legacy by transfer of an asset of equal value from the estate.
Assent	The actual transfer of an asset to the beneficiary by the Personal Representative.
Attest	Declaration in Will where the two witnesses confirm that they have witnessed the Testators signature and signed at the same time and in the presence of the Testator.
Beneficiary	Person who is in receipt of a benefit under a Will.
Bequest	A gift under a Will.
Capital Acquisitions Tax	Tax payable on the taking of a gift or inheritance, usually payable by the recipient.
Capital Gains Tax	Tax payable on the gain arising from the disposal of an asset.
Caveat	A written notice to the Court entered, through the Probate Office, requesting that nothing is done with the Estate of a deceased person, without prior notice to either the party entering the Caveat or to his Solicitor.

Chattels	Movable possessions (as opposed to a house or land).
Citation	Where a person who has an interest in the Estate of a deceased requires the Executor or any other person entitled in priority to a Grant, to prove the Will where they have failed to do so and will not renounce their rights.
Codicil	A supplement to a Will which alters or adds to it.
Contingent Interest	An entitlement under a Will which is subject to an event either happening or not happening.
Demonstrative Legacy	A legacy which is to be paid from the proceeds of a specific asset.
Devise	Gift of real property (e.g. house or land) taken under a Will.
Disclaimer	Where a beneficiary decides not to take their entitlement under a Will they are said to disclaim their benefit. The benefit disclaimed will usually fall into the residue of the estate and be distributed in accordance with the residuary clause provisions.
Discretionary Trust	A Trust where the Trustees have absolute discretion as to how and when they will distribute the Trust Assets to one or more of the Trust's beneficiaries.
Estate	The total Assets and liabilities of a person at date of death.
Executor	Person appointed by Will to administer the Estate of the Testator.
Executors Year	Personal Representative must distribute the estate as soon as possible but proceedings cannot be brought against him before a year after the death of the testator.
Fixed Trust	A Trust where the entitlement of the beneficiaries is clearly defined i.e. fixed.
Grant of Administration with Will annexed	Document issued by the court which confirms the right of the Personal Representative to administer the estate -this issues where there is a Will but where somebody other than an Executor applies for a grant.
Grant of administration intestate	Document issued by the court which confirms the right of the Personal Representative to administer the estate -this issues where a person dies without having made a Will.
Grant of Probate	Document issued by the court which confirms the right of the Executor to administer the Estate.

Grant of Representation	Document issued by the court that enables the Personal Representative to administer the estate of the deceased. This includes:-
	1. Grant of Probate - given only to the Executor of a Will.
	2. Grant of Administration with Will annexed - given where there is a Will but where somebody other than an Executor applies for a Grant.
	3. Grant of Administration Intestate - given where a person dies without having made a Will.
In Specie	In its original form as opposed to the cash equivalent.
Inland Revenue Affidavit	Form which must be submitted to the Revenue Commissioners containing details of the estate including the Assets and liabilities of the Deceased, information on Assets passing outside the Will or intestacy and details of the beneficiaries and the values of the benefits taken.
Intestate	Where a person dies without having made a Will and his Assets are distributed according to Statute.
Lapse	Where a benefit under a Will fails.
Legacy	Gift of personal property taken under a Will; this can be
	specific a gift of a particular asset e.g. a painting, a house etc.
	pecuniary a gift of a cash amount
	demonstrative a gift which is to be paid from the proceeds of a specific asset.
Legal Right Share	Spouse's legal entitlement to a share of the Testators estate which can override the provisions of the Will should the spouse elect to take the legal right share. In cases where a spouse and children survive the testator the spouse is entitled to one third of the estate, if there are no children the spouse is entitled to one half of the estate.
Life interest	An interest in the Income generated by Trust Assets for one's lifetime.
Life Interest Trust	A Trust where one or more beneficiaries (life tenants) are entitled to the Income generated by the Trust Assets and on the happening of a specified event such as the death of the life tenant the Assets of the Trust will be passed out to other named beneficiaries.

Limited Interest	A right to the Income generated by Trust Assets for a limited period.
Per Stirpes	'Through the stocks' - where the beneficiary of a Will is the predeceased child of the Testator, the children of the deceased child shall take their parents entitlement in equal shares.
Personal Property	Movable Assets.
Personal Representative	Person(s) nominated by the testator in his Will to administer an Estate (i.e. executor) or the person(s) appointed by the Court to undertake these duties where a person dies intestate or where someone other than Executors are seeking to prove a Will. (i.e. administrator).
Principal Object	The spouse, children and minor children of a predeceased child of the person who made the Trust.
Probate Office	Office of the court which issues the grant of Probate on receipt of the Will and supporting documents.
Probate Tax	Tax payable on the death of a person; the tax is 2% of the net value of the estate at date of death.
Protective Trust	A Trust established to protect a beneficiary by retaining the Assets on Trust for his/her benefit.
Real Property	Immovable Assets such as a house or lands.
Remainderman	The person entitled to the remainder of the Trust Fund after the termination of the last life interest.
Renunciation of Executor	Where an executor decides not to act in the administration of the estate he confirms his decision by executing a deed of renunciation whereby all rights to participate in the administration of the estate are lost.
Reservation of Executor to act	If an executor decides not to get involved in the administration of the estate he can reserve his right to act at the outset but can at a later stage of the administration become involved.
Residue	The remainder of the estate after payment out of all debts, liabilities and legacies.
Residuary Legatee	A beneficiary under a Will who is entitled to a share or all of the residue.
Revoke	To invalidate a previous Will.

Section 117 Claim	Right of child to contest a parent's will on the grounds that they have not been adequately provided for.
Section 60 Policy	Life assurance policy which is exempt from Inheritance Tax provided the proceeds are used to pay Inheritance Tax.
Statutory notice to Creditors	A notice published in the National press requesting all outstanding creditors of the deceased to present their bills for payment within a stated time frame. This protects the personal representative from the possibility of claims arising after the estate has been distributed.
Succession Act 1965	Act which lays down the succession rules.
Testamentary Expenses	Expenses arising during the course of administration payable by the Executor which includes Probate Tax, valuation fees, legal and accounting fees etc.
Testate	Where a person dies having made a valid Will and his Assets are distributed according to the terms of his Will.
Testator	Person who makes a Will.
Trust	An arrangement that an individual enters into either during his lifetime or in his Will with another person (the Trustee) to hold and deal with certain Assets (the Trust property) in accordance with the individuals' wishes.
Trust for sale	A Trust which requires the Trustee to sell the Trust Assets with power to postpone the sale.
Trustee	A person appointed by a Trust deed to administer a Trust according to the powers, duties and restrictions imposed by law and specifically by the Trust deed.
Trustee Authorised Investments	The range of investments which a Trustee must adhere to in the investment of Trust Assets unless given a wider power of investment in the Trust deed.
Vesting Date	The date on which Assets are legally transferred.
Will	A declaration in writing of the Testators' wishes providing for the distribution of property after his death.